THE SECRET DOCTRINES
OF JESUS

▽ ▽ ▽

The Secret Doctrines of Jesus

BY

H. Spencer Lewis, F. R. C., Ph.D.

Author of
"The Mystical Life of Jesus," "Mansions of the Soul," "The Symbolic Prophecy of the Great Pyramid," "Self Mastery and Fate," "A Thousand Years of Yesterdays," etc.

ROSICRUCIAN LIBRARY
VOLUME IV

SUPREME GRAND LODGE OF AMORC
Printing and Publishing Department
San Jose, California

First Edition, 1937
Copyright 1937 and 1965
by Supreme Grand Lodge of AMORC, Inc.
All Rights Reserved

Library of Congress Catalogue Card No.: 37-22922

ISBN 0-912057-14-9

No part of this publication may be reproduced, stored in a retrieval system, or transmitted, in any form or by any means, electronic, mechanical, photocopying, recording, or otherwise, without prior written permission of the publisher.

Nineteenth Edition, 1981
Third Printing, 1987

Printed and bound in U.S.A.

DEDICATED

to

Sar Hieronymus of Belgium

whose spiritual countenance and purity
of character give boundless charm
to the magnificence of
his wisdom.

▽

The Rosicrucian Library

Volume

- I Rosicrucian Questions and Answers with Complete History of the Order
- II Rosicrucian Principles for the Home and Business
- III The Mystical Life of Jesus
- IV The Secret Doctrines of Jesus
- V Unto Thee I Grant (Secret Teachings of Tibet)
- VI A Thousand Years of Yesterdays (A Revelation of Reincarnation)
- VII Self Mastery and Fate with the Cycles of Life (A Vocational Guide)
- VIII Rosicrucian Manual
- IX Mystics at Prayer
- X Behold the Sign (A Book of Ancient Symbolism)
- XI Mansions of the Soul (A Cosmic Conception)
- XII Lemuria—The Lost Continent of the Pacific
- XIII The Technique of the Master
- XIV The Symbolic Prophecy of the Great Pyramid
- XV The Book of Jasher
- XVI The Technique of the Disciple
- XVII Mental Poisoning
- XXII The Sanctuary of Self
- XXIII Sepher Yezirah
- XXV Son of the Sun
- XXVI The Conscious Interlude
- XXVII Essays of a Modern Mystic
- XXVIII Cosmic Mission Fulfilled
- XXIX Whisperings of Self
- XXX Herbalism Through the Ages
- XXXI Egypt's Ancient Heritage
- XXXII Yesterday Has Much to Tell
- XXXIII The Eternal Fruits of Knowledge
- XXXIV Cares That Infest
- XXXV Mental Alchemy
- XXXVI Messages from the Celestial Sanctum
- XXXVII In Search of Reality
- XXXVIII Through the Mind's Eye
- XXXIX Mysticism—The Ultimate Experience
- XL The Conscience of Science and Other Essays

(Other volumes will be added from time to time.
Write for complete catalogue.)

CONTENTS

▽

		PAGE
	Preface	17
CHAPTER		
I	An Astonishing Discovery	23
II	The Need for Secrecy	33
III	The Great Secret School	39
IV	The Secret Mission of Jesus	61
V	The Stewardship and Discipleship of the Christian Mysteries	73
VI	Individual Secret Missions	97
VII	Strange Biblical Passages	107
VIII	The Greatest of Miracles	133
IX	More Biblical Verification	149
X	The Secret Doctrines	175
XI	The Grand Mysteries	197
XII	Progressive Modifications of the Christian Doctrines	215
XIII	The Preservation of the Secret Teachings	225

SITE OF ANCIENT ESSENES. NEAR THE DEAD SEA IN JORDAN ARE THE RUINS OF THIS ANCIENT DORMITORY AND BANQUET HALL OF THE ESSENES. A SHORT DISTANCE AWAY ARE LOCATED THE HILLS IN THE CAVES OF WHICH WERE FOUND THE FAMED DEAD SEA SCROLLS.
(See page 23).—(*Photo by AMORC*)

THE PLACE OF THE LAST SUPPER. THE TWO WINDOWS, LOWER CENTER, ADMIT LIGHT INTO THE ONCE SECRET COUNCIL CHAMBERS OF JESUS CHRIST.—*(Filmed by AMORC Camera Expedition)*

THE CHURCH OF THE NATIVITY, BETHLEHEM. ALL SECTS AND AUTHORITIES AGREE ON THE AUTHENTICITY OF THIS EDIFICE, THE COURTYARD OF WHICH IS OFTEN USED AS A BARRACKS FOR MODERN TROOPS.—*(Filmed by AMORC Camera Expedition)*

THE MIGHTY WALL AND TOWER OF KING DAVID. THESE SOMBER GRAY STONES OFTEN RESISTED THE SAVAGE ATTACKS OF THE PHILISTINES AND THE OTHER WARLIKE TRIBES OF THE TIMES.
—*(Filmed by AMORC Camera Expedition)*

PREFACE

▽

Argument and controversy are not the primary reasons for writing this book, despite the fact that there is much *argument* in it and that it will unquestionably arouse some *controversy*.

Facts are stubborn things. The truth will reveal itself even when it is hidden behind a veil or intermingled with allegories, parables, and strange interpretations. Most of the facts contained in this book are very clearly revealed in the Christian Bible and particularly in the New Testament. This book, however, is not an example of how the Christian Bible may be misinterpreted or misquoted or promiscuously and arbitrarily quoted in parts to prove an idea, a theory, or a postulation. It has been said that almost any strange theory or staggering proposition can be proved by taking unconnected and unrelated passages from the Bible and piecing them together in such a manner, or giving emphasis to certain words in them, so that they form a new and wholly incorrect representation.

The quotations from the Christian Bible used in this book are surprisingly and strangely illuminating when used precisely as they appear in the

THE SECRET DOCTRINES OF JESUS

New Testament and without separating them from the general text. They contain facts that have been deliberately overlooked or misinterpreted, for they are not susceptible of several interpretations. They either mean something—or nothing at all.

Where the New Testament states that Mary, the mother of Jesus, was one of His secret students or a member of His band of Disciples meeting in a secret place, it does not mean and cannot mean that it was any other Mary, or that she was a member of some other group of students, or that she was merely spiritually or symbolically or allegorically one of His students. It may be very surprising to learn that Jesus had a woman among His members—whether it was Mary His mother or some other woman. But just because it is a surprising fact is no reason to challenge either the truthfulness of it or its implication, its definitely intended meaning, and the significance that lies back of it. If Jesus had His mother, as just a woman, among His private students or secret Disciples or band of Disciples, it is very significant, and not just because she was Mary, His mother. And if this fact is surprising, what then are we to think of the other passages in the New Testament stating that there were other women besides Mary among His private Disciples and that,

THE SECRET DOCTRINES OF JESUS

therefore, all of His Disciples and selected students were not men?

Not that this should be something important enough to write a book about, for after all, women have been eminent students of the great Truths of life, and great teachers and great preachers, and certainly were qualified in those days as they are today to be Disciples equal with men in any and all circumstances. The significance lies in the fact that either the church or its ordained representatives, or some of them, or the Christian movement in the past centuries has deliberately or unconsciously evaded this significant feature of the great work of Jesus the Christ.

The same is true in regard to the brothers and sisters of Jesus being members of His secret, private school. Are we giving too much emphasis to this relationship and to these heretofore veiled incidents of His life? We think not, in the light of the fact that many great sermons have been preached, and pamphlets written, and chapters in books carefully prepared to interpret the attitude of Jesus toward His parents and His flesh-and-blood relatives. Think for a moment of how many millions of times clergymen, in preaching and writing, have attempted to explain the New Testament passage which appears to be a rebuke to His mother on

THE SECRET DOCTRINES OF JESUS

the occasion of His delay at the synagogue. That strange incident has been held before the eyes of Sunday School and Bible students as well as adults as an indication that Jesus had little or no patience with His parents, that they had little or no understanding of His mission in life, and that He could even be unkind, intolerant, and inconsiderate of women and their inquiries concerning His affairs. Such explanations and interpretations have left in the minds of many the doubt as to whether Jesus was as perfect in all human things as He was in all things divine. Is this fair? And are the interpretations of that incident fair in the light of the facts which show that Jesus was broad-minded enough, understanding enough, to allow His mother, brothers, sisters, and other women to be secret, private students of the great "mysteries" which He taught them?

And if it appears that the author of this book is going too far in giving emphasis to any possible secret meetings of a private school of discipleship, let it be kept in mind that the Bible itself is the very best authority for such statements and goes far indeed in giving emphasis to the fact that Jesus taught the multitudes in one manner, taught an outer circle of private students in another manner, and intimately taught and instructed an inner, private school in still another manner. And, we have the repeated statements of Jesus that the great mysteries, the great secrets which He taught to the few in His private discourses and secret meetings, were not susceptible of revelation to the multitudes nor were they susceptible of understanding by the average person. Yet, the Christian church of today fails to make it plain to the masses that there are secrets, there are truths, there are facts, which they do not comprehend because these are difficult to comprehend, but which can be revealed and demonstrated to the worthy, the qualified, and the specially initiated.

These facts give a different coloring to the picture of Christianity as a religious, philosophical, or moral system. In fact, they help us to understand that the original and true Christian instruction, and the original Christian doctrines, were divine things not intended for all human beings; but constituting a system of transcendental truths, of esoteric revelations, and divine laws of unlimited application and omnipotent power. It remains for the challenger of the facts contained in this book to prove his contention. The author sets forth his facts and the truths that are revealed by them. If the quotations used and the facts contained in them reveal truths that are contrary to those contained in this book, then the reader who challenges the book must present his interpretations and show that they are superior to the ones found herein.

Either the many quotations from the New Testament, the many intimations, the many revealing situations and conditions mean something very definite—or they mean nothing at all.

The reader with the open, unbiased mind will be the better judge—

That the Rosicrucian Order throughout the world, the Rosicrucian Brotherhood of AMORC, including its alliances and affiliations, devoted to the perpetuation, the continued revelation, of these ancient truths through carefully guarded dissemination to properly qualified individuals, does not separate the true doctrines of Jesus or His great truths from the original system of Christianity. This book, therefore, is not in essential nature or intent any propaganda for the Rosicrucian Order, AMORC, but a contribution solely to the esoteric literature of thousands of years ago and today.

THE AUTHOR.

Temple of Alden,
Rosicrucian Park,
San Jose, California.
January 20, 1937.

Chapter I
AN ASTONISHING DISCOVERY
▽

O DOUBT most Christians will be surprised at the intimation that Jesus taught secretly any divine principles, or practiced any divine art that He did not reveal to all the world.

The author was astonished when he first discovered that this was true. As a devout attendant at Christian services for thirty years or more, and after many years of Bible reading directed by the leaders of Protestant Christian thought, it seemed to him almost unbelievable that such important facts regarding the life of Jesus, and the early creation of the Christian doctrines and practices, should have been either overlooked by the keenest of the analytical students of Christianity, or deliberately concealed from the public for some reason which might have appeared good and sufficient.

As soon as the key to support these facts revealed itself unmistakably in passages of the New Testament, and unlocked many of the mysteries of the life and activities of Jesus and His Disciples,

THE SECRET DOCTRINES OF JESUS

the numerous puzzling, and even doubtful, passages of the Bible became plain, understandable, and positive evidence in support of the discovery.

In order that the reader may understand and truly comprehend the great secrets which Jesus taught exclusively to His tried and tested Disciples, it is necessary to outline the story revealed by the facts discovered so gradually as to appear to be a truly divine and Cosmic revelation.

Here are the facts: That Jesus had many private and secret meetings or sessions with His Disciples and trusted companions is hinted at in many parts of the New Testament. There is unmistakable evidence of this fact.

That Jesus possessed some rare, secret, divine, or spiritual, as well as semi-scientific knowledge that enabled Him to perform miracles and to convey this secret knowledge and power to others is also unmistakable if we give careful consideration or acceptance to many of the passages in the New Testament.

That the early Christian workers constituting the very foundation of the Christian religion were capable of performing miracles or applying Divine or Cosmic principles in a new and different manner from that which had ever been applied before, is impressed upon our consciousness as we read and analyze the Synoptic Gospels and other parts of the New Testament.

That the early Christian church was devoted to two phases of essential activity—preaching, teaching, postulating, *and* performing, healing, demonstrating—is beyond question.

That the Christian church of today no longer practices or demonstrates those principles of healing or calling upon divine and natural law for unusual manifestations, but concentrates almost exclusively upon preaching and postulating, indicates that the Christian church of today and of the past centuries has either abandoned fully half of its great work, or some secret knowledge possessed by the early Christians has not passed down through the ages from priest to priest, clergyman to clergyman, sect to sect.

The foregoing statements constitute fundamental keys for unlocking the mysteries of the mission of Jesus the Christ while on earth. As a result of a careful study and extensive investigation of the foregoing keys, and the many correlative facts revealed by and through them, the author outlines here the astonishing contentions which he will present in the following chapters of this book:

1. That Jesus the Christ was divinely born, and thus especially prepared—spiritually, mentally and

otherwise—to receive, test, and try certain secret knowledge which would enable Him to carry out a special ministry on earth;

2. That having been properly prepared divinely, spiritually, intellectually, and otherwise for this great mission, it was also decreed that He should dispense this knowledge and convey the special powers which the knowledge developed in Him to others who were well qualified and worthy, in order that they might carry on His mission throughout the ages, and do "even greater things";

3. That during the early years of the ministry of Jesus, He sought, found, trained and prepared those men and women of Palestine, Egypt, and Syria who would be spiritually worthy and morally and ethically qualified to perpetuate the knowledge He brought to earth and the powers that had been conferred upon Him through His divine birth;

4. That these persons so prepared and trained constituted a secret group of adepts and companion workers assembling from time to time as a secret college for instruction, test, trial, and critical practice of the secret principles;

5. That such a secret society was formed by Jesus, and maintained in continuous functioning and action throughout the last years of the life of

THE SECRET DOCTRINES OF JESUS

Jesus, and did not become extinct at the time of the Crucifixion and Ascension;

6. That the men and women bound by secret oaths into this secret society numbered one hundred and twenty, it not being limited to just His twelve Apostles or Disciples, and that this astonishing and startling fact is clearly stated in the New Testament;

7. That like any other secret society that had to guard carefully its teachings, principles, membership list, and ideals and purposes against political or aristocratic persecution, this mysterious body of divine students had several definite, fixed, continuously-used meeting places in Jerusalem with branches for occasional meetings in outlying districts;

8. That its principal meeting place or "Temple" was well guarded and well protected, known by a secret name, and known only to the tried and tested members—a fact also proved by very definite passages in the New Testament;

9. That the secret society also had passwords, signs, symbols, and other tokens by which the members recognized one another, and prevented spies or political persecutors from joining them or becoming acquainted with their secret work—which is also proved by quotations from the New Testament;

THE SECRET DOCTRINES OF JESUS

10. That when the members of this secret society were called together by Jesus on regular and special occasions they had to approach their secret meeting place one by one with the greatest care and be guided by secret signs which were changed from period to period;

11. That among the one hundred and twenty members were not only those who were later known as the Twelve Disciples and who constituted the secret executive committee of this secret society, but also others who were interested in the mysterious, secret work of the society, including the mother of Jesus and His brothers and sisters;

12. That during the course of study and preparation for the secret work Jesus not only taught them the secret lessons, but aided them in developing within their own beings the same mysterious, secret, spiritual power which He possessed, and once having accomplished this and having made them ready in every way, He conferred upon them the divine authority to use the special power they had developed and to represent Him and the Kingdom of Heaven throughout the future centuries;

13. That among the one hundred and twenty secret students were wealthy men of the country, and a few who possessed political influence and power, and who later came to the aid of Jesus in

THE SECRET DOCTRINES OF JESUS

His hours of persecution and performed certain acts which they had all promised one another to do in case of such an emergency;

14. That the parables and allegorical instructions which Jesus gave to the public, and particularly to those of the public who followed Him more or less carefully, were veiled and deliberately concealed secret truths which cannot be understood and properly interpreted today unless one possesses an outline of the secret teachings given to His secret student body;

15. That this special secret society may or may not have been affiliated with the Essenes—another secret society with which Jesus was well acquainted;*

16. That each of the secret teachings constitutes a divine law spiritually applied and materially manifested, and that each is outlined in almost perfect detail—hidden in parts of the New Testament—and can be pieced together for complete and perfect understanding;

17. That these secret teachings and practices are missing in the instructions of the Christian church today, and because some of these secret truths have been discovered by those outside of the Christian church, various sects and cults

* See footnote, page 31.

THE SECRET DOCTRINES OF JESUS

utilizing this secret knowledge have come into existence as rivals of the Christian church;

18. That if the Christian church of today would make itself learned in this secret knowledge, and spend time in teaching, preparing, and qualifying certain devout students of each section of the world to practice and demonstrate this secret knowledge, it would become the most potent, powerful influence for peace, happiness, health, and contentment. It could do way with most of the other problems of life and bring about the Kingdom of Heaven on earth with the gradual elimination of national and international war, strife, contests, and personal error and sin.

All of the foregoing facts will be presented in the succeeding chapters of this book. The foregoing synopsis represents the author's postulations and theme. Undoubtedly it will be rejected by the average clergyman, pastor, or priest, and scoffed at by the average devout Christian. Strange as it may seem, however, the followers of so-called heathen, pagan, or non-Christian religions will be among the first to recognize the truth of this book, and to bring forth from their own experiences in life, and from their archives, bits of evidence to support it. And those of Christian birth or inclination who have gradually wandered

THE SECRET DOCTRINES OF JESUS

away from the Christian path, or the Christian church, will hail this book as a correct explanation of what they conceive to be a weakness in the Christian church today, and a good reason for their delinquency and indifference in support of Christian institutions.

To the students of mysticism, metaphysics, mystical philosophy, and Cosmic law—such as Rosicrucians, Theosophists, Freemasons, Hermeticists, and Martinists—this book will be welcome, and supported by the most common incidents of their lives and the ancient records of their organizations.

---
* Footnote.

In recent years the discovery of the Dead Sea Scrolls has confirmed the author's reference to the Essenes and their secret teachings which preceded Christianity and with which Jesus must have been well acquainted. A partial news report on the findings of such archeologists as English-born G. Lankester Harding, Director of the Jordanian Department of Antiquities, is as follows:

"Most startling disclosure of the Essene documents so far published is that the sect possessed, years before Christ, a terminology and practice that have always been considered uniquely Christian. The Essenes practiced baptism and shared a liturgical repast of bread and wine presided over by a priest. They believed in redemption and in the immortality of the soul. Their most important leader was a mysterious figure called the Teacher of Righteousness, a Messianic prophet-priest blessed with divine revelation, persecuted and perhaps eventually martyred."

"Many phrases, symbols and precepts similar to those in Essene literature are used in the New Testament, particularly in the Gospel of John and the Pauline Epistles. John the Baptist's use of baptism has led some scholars to believe that he was either an Essene or strongly influenced by the sect. The scrolls have also given fresh impetus to the theory that Jesus may have been a student of Essene thought. It is notable that the New Testament never once mentions the Essenes, though it casts frequent aspersions on the two other leading sects, the Sadducees and the Pharisees."—Publisher

Chapter II

THE NEED FOR SECRECY

▽

THE first question that naturally arises in the minds of the devout Christian and the sincere student of the Bible is, "Was there any need for a secret instructor and the preservation of secret knowledge in connection with the mission of Jesus?"

A second question might be, "If it is conceded that Jesus was divinely ordained to be the Saviour of mankind, as well as the teacher and instructor of those who sought eternal life through divine truths, why was He made to preserve the knowledge and power in such secrecy and to convey it only to a few?"

We hear similar questions asked today by those who are prejudiced toward churches of all denominations, and who believe that God should have revealed all knowledge to all mankind, and should continue to reveal such knowledge, and confer extraordinary spiritual and worldly powers upon all individuals, and thus bring about more rapidly and more surely a Kingdom of Heaven on earth.

THE SECRET DOCTRINES OF JESUS

Looking back through history we find that on scores of occasions, dating back into great antiquity, God has inspired certain wise and select characters to be revelators or avatars, and to teach and preach such knowledge as would lift the consciousness of man to a higher plane and make his understanding and comprehension broader, and bring him closer in his attunement with the principles of eternal life and truth. Each of these great Lights has contributed to the advancement of civilization, and to the moral development of man. But the process was slow and lacked efficiency. The increasing population of the world, accompanied by an increasing demoralizing influence of a satanic nature, and the rapid deterioration of sound principles that make for stabilized morality among men and women, necessitated the sending to earth of a Saviour who would found or organize and maintain a permanent system of guidance and instruction that would reach throughout the world.

It is a fundamental truth, as true today as it was two thousand years ago, that not all of mankind is prepared or ready or qualified in any sense to receive or to comprehend and use the higher truths of life and the miraculous power that comes from such knowledge. God must have seen, as He must see today, that until the individual becomes worthy spiritually, as well as intellectually and socially, he neither deserves nor can he absorb and properly apply the greater truths that make man free and start him on the path of eternal life. The very experiences of Jesus in carrying out His mission give us excellent reasons for the principle of secrecy. Even among those who were carefully tested and prepared and qualified, there were those who became doubters, those who sought to use the knowledge and power for personal and selfish purposes, and who became spies and enemies, as well as traitors to the cause.

The persecution as well as the prosecution that came to Jesus point out an excellent reason for the principle of secrecy.

While it is true that the mission of Jesus ended early, just as He was reaching the prime of manhood; and while it is true that every conceivable thing was done by the prosecutors and persecutors to destroy the knowledge and power that Jesus had brought to mankind, vestiges of the truth and faint elements of the miraculous power He conferred have come down to us through the ages and have been the means of man's gradual redemption. Had it not been for the system of secrecy, had it not been for the secret organization, the careful test and trial of each who has been the guardian of the great mysteries, the Great Light which came to earth in the first thirty years of the Christian Era would have gone out at the time of the Ascension of Jesus the Christ, and today the teachings and practices which He made so magnificently real and universally applicable to the needs of man, would have been lost, and mankind would have fallen back into the errors of the past and the world would be today without the faintest glimmer of that Great Light.

The early Christian church, after the passage of the "keys" from St. Peter to the next and successive Christian leaders, maintained that it actually carefully preserved for a century or two the spirit of the early secret organization founded by Jesus. The history of the early activities of the Christian church shows that while the populace constituted a large outer circle of worshipers and students of the Christian teachings, they were given only a veiled and very carefully moderated form of the Christian principles; and in a secret inner circle, of a limited number, probationers were led step by step through the higher secret mysteries and teachings to a degree of development and unfoldment where they could carry on the work that Jesus had started and which He transmitted to His Disciples.

THE SECRET DOCTRINES OF JESUS

But, as the centuries passed, the secret teachings became more and more exclusive, while the allegories and incomprehensible principles of veiled instruction became distorted, ritualized, and aborted in the darkened minds of the masses.

It is unquestionably true that in the archives of the Holy Roman Catholic Church, and in the hearts and minds of its great, sincere, and saintly leaders of the past centuries, the true secret teachings and divine powers transferred by Jesus have been preserved, and are conscientiously used in limited ways for the upbuilding of the strength of that church and the protection of its high authority. But it is equally true that among the rank and file of Christian fellowship today, both Roman Catholic and Protestant, this great secret knowledge is unknown and even unsuspected. We see, therefore, that in every real sense the keys to the Church of Christ —which Jesus transmitted to Peter as the leader of His great school of Disciples—were actual keys indeed, and that the keys which should pass from each successor of Peter to the next preserver and expounder of truth, are not mere allegorical keys, but golden keys that unlock the gates—that open the portals—to all of the Christian temples and tabernacles, to all of the hearts and souls, and to all of the schools of life that exist today.

Chapter III
THE GREAT SECRET SCHOOL

▽

HAVING discovered the keys that confirmed the existence of the secret society, it was not difficult to turn to ancient archives and records, to historical and Scriptural writings outside of the Christian Bible, and to many passages in the New Testament which, when put together like the Rosary beads on a string, give us a very definite picture of the manner in which Jesus proceeded to fulfill His great mission in life.

In the first place it should be kept in mind that there was ample precedent to guide Jesus in the matter of organizing a worldly, physical body such as the secret group we are describing. Throughout the preceding centuries there had been in Egypt, India, Persia, and other sections of the Near East, secret schools and movements devoted to the preservation and perpetuation of revealed wisdom. In most of the progressive countries of the Near East there was an official state priesthood devoted to the spread of the state religion and the preservation of the religious traditions and

THE SECRET DOCTRINES OF JESUS

beliefs of antiquity. There were also in each of these countries one or more secret organizations composed of freethinkers, philosophers, illumined mystics, and religious devotees who sought for the truth regarding the mysteries of life and preferred the spiritual and Cosmic revelations that came to them as a blessing from God and a gift to mankind, and, little by little, cast aside the ancient traditions, superstitions, and mythological beliefs of their ancestors. Therefore, in all lands there had been for many centuries a contest between the seekers for revealed truth and the protectors of the older and false forms of religion.

As might be expected, the state priesthood had every physical and worldly advantage in forcing its beliefs and practices upon the populace while the seekers, skeptics, heretics, and the illumined ones found it necessary often to sacrifice their lives and all of their worldly belongings to preserve the greater truths that had been revealed to them or which they had discovered through the use of revealed keys.

The bitter fight between the cult of Amenhotep IV and the established priesthood of Egypt is a typical example of this continuous contest between Light and Darkness. The great illumination that had come to the Pharaoh Amenhotep IV, making plain to him for the first time in the history of civilization the truthful principles of the existence of but one ever-living God, and the falsity of a multiplicity of gods, constituted an awakening and a shocking reaction throughout his country. It was inevitable that although he gave his time and his fortune and his very best interests to the development of this new revelation, this monotheistic religion, and built temples and shrines to the everlasting God, and destroyed those statues, temples, tablets, and walls that adhered to the older beliefs, his life would be taken and the crafty priesthood would be successful in the overthrow of what it considered a dangerous rival movement. And although the Pharaoh suffered intensely and was brought to an early transition, the young man had accomplished so much in the nation-wide spread of his religion that hundreds and even thousands of years have not dimmed the brilliancy of his doctrines and prayers to the God of all creatures; nor have they been lost to posterity.

After Jesus had received the Baptism, and the Holy Ghost had come down upon Him, filling His very being with that divine wisdom and power that transformed Him from a soul incarnate in the flesh of the world into a Christ to redeem the world, He could not have failed to realize that

THE SECRET DOCTRINES OF JESUS

each revelation, each divine urge, each vision, each spoken message that came to Him from the lips of angels or from God Himself, was leading Him along the same path of suffering, intrigue, treachery, and ultimate crucifixion that all of His predecessors had witnessed in their careers as Lights among men.

The records of the activities of all preceding leaders of divine thought, and creators of secret organizations to preserve and perpetuate the divine teachings, must have furnished Jesus with an excellent map and an impressive picture of the path He must take in working out His ordained mission.

I shall not touch upon the preliminary education and training which Jesus must have received even as a young boy to make Him so brilliant of mind in His twelfth year that He astonished the Elders of the Synagogue of His country, nor shall I refer to the higher worldly, as well as spiritual, education that came to Him as a young man during the beginning of His mission and which enabled Him to deal in allegories, analogies, and metaphors related to the personal affairs, occupations, interests, desires, hopes, and trials and tribulations of peoples in many distant nations, in many trades, occupations, and professions, and in many private walks of life. The young man born to a carpenter of

THE SECRET DOCTRINES OF JESUS

very mediocre circumstances could not have acquired all of this knowledge in the primitive schools of His own land, and He could not have been sent to any very distant country to attend a private school of training, because of lack of funds. The preparation which He had as a youth and then as a young man was not solely the result of inspired visions and messages coming to Him through the Cosmic from the consciousness of God, for His development, training, and education were of a dual nature. He was familiar with the customs and habits, the deceits, the hypocritical beliefs, the worldly temptations and weaknesses of peoples of many lands, and He seemed to possess a limitless knowledge of spiritual and divine laws and of great Cosmic truths which He could not have learned except by placing Himself wholly and enthusiastically in harmony with God His Father who ordained that He should go forth from the Heavenly Kingdom to the kingdom of earth and transform it into a land of peace as the Kingdom of Heaven on earth.

There can be no question of His spiritual education, preparation, and illumination in regard to the higher things of life. It was unquestionably revealed wisdom, revealed religion, and revealed law. From no other source could such wisdom come. But it is equally true that His worldly knowledge, so minutely comprehended in its true relationship to the worldly things of life, as shown in His hundreds of allegories and metaphors, could have been attained in no other way than through personal contact with these worldly situations, with these worldly people and their worldly ideas.

The early education of Jesus (known as "Joseph" until His baptism) is fully covered in my previous book, *The Mystical Life of Jesus*, and there is no need for further reference to the importance of this early training. But we must not overlook the fact that part of this early training included the study of the trials and successes, the failures and the hopes and aspirations of those who had formed or organized or supported secret schools and movements in other nearby lands, and who had done so with more or less the same purpose in mind as must have moved Jesus at times when He had a keen realization of the spiritual contacts that were being made by Him and of the obligations He would soon have to assume.

We are not surprised, therefore, to find that in carrying out His Father's wishes and organizing a secret society, and in protecting it and advancing it, Jesus resorted to and utilized many of the points and principles of organization which were then

THE SECRET DOCTRINES OF JESUS

already established among secret schools in the Near and Far East. Even some of the terminology and secret symbols which Jesus used and to which He referred in a veiled manner in His conversations, preachments, and allegorical stories, were identical with those of other schools and instantly recognized by members of foreign or distant secret movements, and these are the same today in many ways.

And so we find from a careful examination of the old records in various archives of the Near East where references to Jesus are still carefully preserved, and from isolated and specially emphasized passages in the New Testament, that soon after His Baptism and the influx of the Holy Ghost which began His mission in life, He mixed with the rich and the poor, the good and the bad, the cultured and the publicans, the righteous and the sinners, and gained much from their conversations and from their discussions of the fixed or established religious customs of the day. Possessing a keen insight, and a special divine gift of intuitive reception of knowledge from the mind of God or man, and having only honesty to serve and truth to reveal, He gradually gathered together in the olive groves and in the open spaces along the great highways of Palestine those men and women who

THE SECRET DOCTRINES OF JESUS

showed any inclination toward listening to Him while He preached. And at the close of a brief period of instruction He would suddenly ask questions of His hearers as though desiring to have them argue with Him or discuss the important points, but always with the idea of learning how the mind of man was assimilating and accepting the rational and futuristic principles which He claimed were necessary for man's salvation. Because of political opposition, and knowing what had happened in past centuries, He held nearly all of His preliminary meetings for testing and selecting worthy disciples in the open spaces adjoining the highway, where the Roman soldier, the Jewish official, and the suspicious Arab or others could observe what He said and discover no technical error, no crime against the state, no gross insult against the established religions, and no violation of the military regulations.

At first many scoffed at His broad and positive statements that were like proclamations and prophecies, while others smiled at His descriptions of the misery that would come into the lives of the wealthy and the rich, the lazy and the neglectful. The learned men of the synagogue, the religious rulers, the political controllers, smiled in ridicule at the growth and development of His little

THE SECRET DOCTRINES OF JESUS

band of followers. He was looked upon as a harmless radical or a harmless extremist who might catch and hold the interest of a few for a few minutes. But to those who were sincere and those who in every generation and period of time constitute the real seekers for truth, there was something strange and mystical about His manner of delivery, about His method of performing a demonstration of the simple but mysterious laws of nature.

So it was not long before Jesus found Himself surrounded by two classes of men and women— the doubters and scoffers, and those who believed in Him and His teachings but were fearful of their own lives in being sincere either among those who were for or against Him.

Jesus soon found it necessary to carry on His work in a twofold or dual manner. It was necessary to continue the open meetings, the open demonstrations and performances of miracles along the highways in the presence of the multitudes, but it was also necessary for Him to meet, at various times of each month, His honest and sincere co-workers whom He had carefully selected in past months to carry on His great work. Here is where Jesus found the experiences of previous avatars and leaders of great value, and the records would

THE SECRET DOCTRINES OF JESUS

indicate that He did not deviate very greatly from the methods used by them when it came to the details of physical, worldly recognition.

Evidently there were two types among the men and women whom He admitted into His secret schools or into His secret meeting places. The first of these constituted those who were sincerely anxious to know the facts but who deliberately took these facts with a grain of salt and who demanded from time to time signs and demonstrations. They became sincere students as far as a desire to master the principles of these demonstrations was concerned, for such mastery would enable them to go forth and heal the sick and make the lame walk and the blind see as Jesus had done, but they were not anxious to follow His spiritual precepts and to change the course of their personal lives so that they might become of that ideal state which Jesus held forth as the ultimate goal of His mission.

There was a second class who accepted in sincere faith all of the great truths postulated by Jesus and who cared naught, or very little, for continuous demonstrations of His power, finding in the virtue of their improved lives all the reward that they sought.

THE SECRET DOCTRINES OF JESUS

These two factions within His group of followers caused Him to go to many extremes to impress upon them the importance of the work which He had to do and which He realized had to be continued by these followers in future years.

It was no easy task that Jesus had in organizing such an institution or school as He visioned, and we have ample evidence that He went into loneliness or *into the silence* on many occasions and wept and prayed and asked God for special guidance. The sins of the world did not sadden Him nearly as greatly as did the indifference and the insincerity of those who were truly worthy of becoming His great Disciples but who still held fast to the pleasures of the world and who could not give themselves wholly and completely to the new movement.

But we find that as time passed He selected one hundred and twenty of His followers and students to be actual members of His secret society. There were those whom He had to cast aside and leave in the outer circle of membership representing the casual or the insincere seeker for truth. We have the same class of individuals today going hither and thither to listen to the words of wisdom of great preachers and orators, buying books and manuscripts, ever seeking, as they claim, the great

THE SECRET DOCTRINES OF JESUS

truths of life. But in the sanctums of their own hearts and in the still hours of their own meditations and self-examinations, they classify the truths they have received and analyze them in the light of their own previous beliefs and especially in the light of their own most convenient beliefs and convictions. They create a philosophy, a code of life, a religious doctrine, or a creed of their own which is an intermingling of their own beliefs and those which they have found it convenient and possible to accept from the hearts and minds of others. They never really discover or comprehend and inwardly understand the great truths which they are seeking. They close their lives still sure that the one great teacher who could have revealed to them all the truths that they could accept and which would be unmistakably proved to them, had not made his appearance, and that *somewhere* this great teacher still lived while they sought here and there, daily passing by the portal of the temple they hoped to find.

In order that the unworthy and those who had been in the outer circle of fellowship might not participate in the secret instructions and divine revelations that God had promised Jesus would be given to His Disciples, it was only natural that Jesus should have planned that He and His one hundred and twenty tried and tested and duly qualified companions should meet secretly in some definite place and should have some sign or word or token by which they might identify themselves.

And so in the very heart of Jerusalem, in a street where it would not have been suspected, and where protection against annoyance from the Roman soldiers was guaranteed, they acquired and maintained a secret meeting place which had a very vague name and was known only to Jesus and the one hundred and twenty associated members.

All of this may seem like a bit of fiction or imagination and invention, but I shall show a little later on that these statements are facts supported by unquestionable proof found in the New Testament in phrases, paragraphs, and words that could have no other interpretation or meaning and which have appeared strange and mysterious to students of the Bible heretofore.

And so on certain nights, according to the phases of the moon and the regulation of the Jewish and Roman holidays, with which they did not want to conflict and thereby draw attention to themselves, and in harmony with the ancient customs of previous avatars who knew the value of the harmonics and beneficent aspects of the heav-

THE SECRET DOCTRINES OF JESUS

enly and Cosmic conditions, these one hundred and twenty students and their divine Leader met on stated occasions without any special notification; and on special occasions, because of an emergency or because of some great revelation that had come to Jesus during the day or at night, they would be called together by a cryptic message passed among them.

It was in this way that Jesus gradually unfolded to His selected pupils the great secret truths of the mysteries of life and of death, of the spiritual values here on earth and the spiritual values of the Kingdom to come. It was at these meetings that He proved and demonstrated to them that His doctrines were not alone philosophical, religious, moral, nor merely of value ethically, but of practical value in dealing with the affairs of life. He taught them the nature of disease and its cause, and the cure of all disease. He taught them the fallacy of exclusive dependence upon drugs or herbs, witchcraft, incantations and other things when there was a great divine power that could and would exert itself through them, and which had in it as its essential element the creative power that God used in the beginning of time in the creation of the universe and all that existed on or above or below the surface of the earth. The changing

THE SECRET DOCTRINES OF JESUS

of water into wine, the giving forth of blood from stone, the instant knitting of broken bones and torn tissues, the restoration of impulse in the lifeless heart, the giving of light and sight to the darkened eyes, the making of bread and manna from the invisible elements of space, and hundreds of similar demonstrations of natural and divine law working in unison, were parts of the procedure at each one of these secret meetings. The way to eternal life, the true immortality of the soul, the purification of the *body* and the *self within,* the attainment of spiritual beauty, divine power and attunement with God were explained carefully, step by step, in class lessons and personal instruction. The Law of the Triangle and the significance of the Trinity were fundamental in all of the philosophical discussions and in all of the alchemical or physical demonstrations of God's universal laws.

We can close our eyes and see, possibly with the vision of the mystic, the most important meeting place. It must have been quite large indeed to have accommodated one hundred and twenty-one persons with ample room for demonstrations. We know positively that this room was set aside for a long period of time for the exclusive use of Jesus and His students and that it had a significant name, a name that meant something very definite to the Disciples but has evidently meant little to the students of Christianity in the passing centuries. We may see a little later that the name of this room would furnish one of the important keys to the situation, although as a key it has been overlooked throughout the past nineteen hundred years. Most of the secret temples and meeting places of the mystic philosophers in past centuries had been in grottoes or in ruined subterranean spaces where safety was assured and where silence was an important factor. A few such meeting places, however, had been above the ground and even above the first story of some old structure, and we find in this particular case that Jesus and His Disciples had selected a large room above the first floor where the passers-by on the streets of Jerusalem would have suspected nothing, especially if the Disciples carried out the rigid instructions of entering the old structure one by one while a guard secretly watched the street and gave warning of an approaching passer-by. With the windows heavily curtained but with the ceiling open in a large square to the heavenly stars above, an altar in the center with candles upon it to give sufficient illumination, no degree of the light could be seen from the street.

THE SECRET DOCTRINES OF JESUS

Perhaps the most astonishing thing about this society and its meetings is the fact that when Jesus selected, very carefully and undoubtedly with spiritual guidance and revelation, the one hundred and twenty worthy ones whom He could entrust with His very life, He included His own mother and His brothers and sisters. I say it is astonishing not because He found His mother or His brothers and sisters worthy, but because the average student of the Bible and the average devout Christian will question this fact and say it is impossible because it is not revealed by the word of God in the Bible. But the truth of the matter is that it is revealed in the New Testament and so definitely that it cannot be questioned. It is to be found in several passages which I shall quote later and it makes plain and understandable other incidents of relationship between Jesus and His parents connected with His life mission, which are not understandable without a knowledge of this association with Jesus in the secret society. In fact, there are many Christians who will read this book and who will deny that Jesus had brothers and sisters. I have heard my statement in this regard challenged so often in public lectures and in Sunday night discussions in churches that I have found it easy to turn rapidly to various parts of the New

THE SECRET DOCTRINES OF JESUS

Testament and read the positive statements to an astonished congregation.

Is it any wonder, then, that the average Christian student of the Bible is so unfamiliar with much of the secret work of Jesus during His earthly mission?

If the Bible can be read by so many millions and analyzed by so many learned preachers and interpreters, and if so much can be written and expounded about the life of Jesus without making it generally realized that Jesus had brothers and sisters who were born after Him—if we are to believe many passages in the Bible—or some born before Him and some after Him if we are to believe other records—then we should not be surprised that the real, secret purpose, the real, secret laws, ideals, and doctrines of Jesus should have become lost to Christians of modern times.

Jesus continued with His students and with His secret school until the last hour of His life. He had told his pupils over and over again what the great teachers of all ages have told the sincere pupil, that a time would come when perfection or mastership would descend as from Heaven and rest upon them as a result of their devotion to their studies and their patience with their lessons and performances. Jesus assured His Disciples that the

THE SECRET DOCTRINES OF JESUS

time would come when God would fulfill His promise and have the Holy Ghost descend upon them as it had upon Him, and that with this benediction from God, He, as their master-teacher, would also give them authority to go out into the world and not only teach and preach as He had done, but perform the miracles that He had performed and do even greater things. Year after year these students looked forward to this greatest of all graduation exercises, this greatest of all graduation days, when the miracle of miracles would be performed in their behalf. But Jesus had warned them also that before this might occur He would have to descend into hell and carry His cross, sacrifice His earthly life, be crucified and buried. He knew from the lives of the previous Lights of the world, from the prophecies of the great patriarchs, from the visions that God had revealed to Him, that He must suffer this persecution at the hands of the very ones He would help and that He would be betrayed by one He trusted; and that again, as in thousands of instances in the story of past civilization, one traitor must be found in the midst of the true and loyal to exemplify the spirit of darkness and the character of Satan.

And then came the dark hour and all that had been anticipated and prophesied was fulfilled.

THE SECRET DOCTRINES OF JESUS

Silently the majority of His students, pledged by their very lives to secrecy, stood back from the hordes of gossiping spectators with that understanding that the others could never attain, and watched the dramatic performance and fulfillment of the old Cosmic principle that the great Master must carry His cross to the place of persecution and suffer upon it and be entombed as of the dead and thus be prepared for His ultimate ascension into the Kingdom of perfect peace and love. The special twelve students who represented His bodyguard and executive board, and who were to be known to the world as His only secret followers, performed their proper duties during the hours of His suffering while the hundred or more, including His mother, performed their silent duties, always mindful of the watchful eye of the enemy. And one of the richest of His secret members came forward—as though suddenly inspired—and offered to care for the body at just the timely moment when the law had been decreed that this duty should be fulfilled.

Then the curtain closed and dropped upon this great scene without the soldiers and the politicians, the scoffers, the critics, and those who had thrown stones and who had spat upon Him ever knowing that a band of a hundred and twenty had surrounded that theater of Golgotha, making a mystic circle, the power of which raised Jesus beyond human injury or human defilement; that instead of this being the final act and the closing of the tomb bringing an end to the career of a mysterious miracle worker, it was merely the temporary closing of a tomb that would be opened again and from which would arise the great Redeemer of mankind whose power had ascended while He was upon the Cross but would descend again, not upon one, but upon the mystical number of one hundred and twenty; that through this transformation of the man Jesus and the transference of His power, there would be brought into the world the beginning of a new Kingdom that would be eternal on earth.

▽

CHAPTER IV
THE SECRET MISSION OF JESUS

▽

CONSTANT reference has been made in the preceding chapters to the great mission which Jesus was to carry out in His lifetime on earth. Since that mission seemed to be so greatly associated with all the essentials of secrecy and mystery, it may be well to pause for the moment and give that mission itself some consideration.

We have already referred to the fact that throughout the preceding centuries illuminated characters had arisen upon the horizon and shed light and divine revelations among the peoples of various nations. Even when we hesitate to accept at face value the strange statements found in the mythological records of ancient philosophies and religions, and even when we greatly discount the allegorical statements found in the history of the Egyptian and Hindu religions, for instance, we still have a mass of facts which plainly indicate that the populace of these countries believed for many centuries that the great leaders who arose among them and led them out of spiritual darkness

THE SECRET DOCTRINES OF JESUS

into light, were divinely born and divinely ordained to carry out a mission of illumination.

As was pointed out in my book dealing with the mystical life of Jesus, there were many such characters in behalf of whom claims were made of immaculate conception or divine conception and birth, and there are recorded incidents that almost parallel the stories of the conception and birth of Jesus. Even if we do not accept these statements in past records as true, but merely as allegorical, we must come to the conclusion that it was a common belief among the peoples of ancient times that these mystic philosophers and illuminated "wise men" were the representation of their god or gods, and had been uniquely as well as spiritually appointed and ordained to appear among men at various stages of developing civilization to point out the next path, or the next higher path, and the better way to journey out of their present situation into better and more noble ones. And we can easily understand how the admiring and adoring, and even worshipful, followers in each cycle of time invented or created exaggerated or fantastic stories about the extreme divinity and uniqueness of these "wise men" after these leaders had passed on. We are given in this day to making extraordinary heroes out of those who achieve any kind

THE SECRET DOCTRINES OF JESUS

of greatness in any field of earthly endeavor, and we still have a tendency to look upon every greatly illuminated mind as having been not only ordained to fulfill a mission of illumination, but as having been unique in even a physical, mental, and biological sense.

This tendency of attributing to the wise and illuminated leaders of mankind certain distinctive qualities not common to all mankind is still carried out, for instance, among Christian worshipers who feel that each of the Disciples of Jesus must have been Cosmically conceived as a soul, and physically born on the earth plane in a unique manner to have attained the great heights and the noble position which they occupy in the Christian religion. Despite the fact that Christian literature and Christian records tell us, for instance, that St. Matthew, before his conversion to Christianity, was a publican or a tax gatherer residing at Capernaum, and that after becoming a great preacher and a great light among men—leaving several spiritual records that will remain immortal in the Christian Bible—he died a natural death, Christians seem to feel that he is deserving of the title of Saint, not because of the good he accomplished in the latter part of his life as a Disciple and missionary, but because of some unique quali-

THE SECRET DOCTRINES OF JESUS

ties which must have been assigned to his soul and his personality before that soul projected from the Kingdom of Heaven, or Cosmic space, into the little physical body born on earth, and that even his birth must have been attended by some unique incidents or conditions not common to all mankind.

Despite the fact that Christian records tell us very definitely, and without any attempt to paint any fantastic picture, that Saint Mark was really one by the name of John whose surname was Mark, and despite the fact that little is known of his personal life before his conversion to Christianity, and no event is attributed to him that would have attracted to him the attention of the public before he began to preach as an associate of the other Disciples, Christians tend to visualize him as a devout and holy child growing into magnificent spiritual manhood, preordained to be a great light in the Christian church, and a saint. And so with all of the characters associated with the Christian history.

But one thing is certain in connection with the ancient records regarding the avatars and great lights that preceded Jesus—they did fulfill a mission in life, regardless of whether or not it was divinely ordained, or they were uniquely born. It

THE SECRET DOCTRINES OF JESUS

is not because these ancient mystic philosophers and wise men pretended or claimed to be divinely sent that contemporary history and modern history acclaim them as divinely inspired and appointed to a life mission of uniqueness, but because of what they actually accomplished and did for developing civilization, and because of the illumination and light they shed among men.

In studying and analyzing the writings or teachings of these ancient philosophers we find revealed truth and inspired wisdom constituting the theme of their continuous contributions to the moral and spiritual thought of the day. Whence came this wonderful knowledge, and what is it that can lift a man out of an ordinary position in life and cause him to cast aside all of the opportunities for personal comfort and selfish attainment—to work diligently and long in behalf of the spiritual, or at least the moral and ethical—to make every human sacrifice to uplift mankind and to suffer bravely the final and ultimate reward which humanity seems insistent upon giving to those who help it the most? For, history clearly records that most of these Illuminated Ones of the past suffered the treachery, the suspicion, the jealousy, and envy of certain sects and classes of people of their time, and in most cases passed through transition as glorified

THE SECRET DOCTRINES OF JESUS

beings, hanged upon an allegorical cross at least, and mocked by those who should have been most appreciative of their accomplishments.

Nothing but some Cosmically arranged plan, some divinely preordained scheme, some idea conceived by God and authorized by Him, could be responsible for the unique position which these ancient philosophers occupied in their time, and for the great wisdom which they gave to the world, and left in impressive records. These recorded teachings of these philosophers clearly show that the revelations of the great truths of life not only came from a divine source through special messages and visions, promptings and urges, but the truths thus revealed and presented to the mass of mankind were progressive and were as steps leading onward and upward toward the higher planes of existence and conscious understanding. Each one of these avatars seemed to lay a foundation and then build upon it a structure that rose until it lifted the consciousness of mankind to a point or plane where it could rise no higher in that cycle of the development of civilization and spiritual progress on earth.

Then, after a long period of silence, another avatar would appear and would carry the development on to another higher plane. In analyzing the

THE SECRET DOCTRINES OF JESUS

teachings of these ancient mystics and wise men, we find that the last of them had brought the unfoldment of spiritual consciousness, and moral and ethical comprehension of man, up to a point where mankind was ready for the surprising and startling truths and principles which Jesus revealed in even His earliest discourses. When Jesus stated to His sincere followers that He brought them a New Way to eternal life, that He brought them a realization and fulfillment of the prophecies of the wise men of the past, He meant precisely what He said, and the development of Christianity and Christian principles has revealed to us, in the nineteen hundred or more years which have passed, that perhaps He spoke more wisely than He knew, or that He did know whereof He spoke because of His prior preparation and training for the ministry and mission of His life.

What, then, was that mission? Was it to be like unto the missions of the preceding wise men and Illuminated ones? Was He merely to rise in the darkness of the cycle of time and lift the consciousness of mankind one degree higher as His predecessors had done, and save mankind from faltering on its way, or returning to its ancient beliefs and practices? Was He, after all, to be but another one of the divinely inspired

THE SECRET DOCTRINES OF JESUS

and preordained Saviours of the passing cycles of time?

No matter how we may view His ancestry and the immediate conditions surrounding His physical conception and birth, the fact remains that Jesus, as the newest and greatest of divine Lights, arose in the midst of a people seemingly unneedful of a new religion or a higher religion, or a more sincere religion. If we analyze the Jewish religion which surrounded Him on the one hand, we find that aside from some beliefs which Christians look upon today as perhaps wanting in sincerity, there is no question about the general sincerity of all the followers of the Jewish religion, and particularly regarding their adoration of "the one ever-living God." And if we analyze the other religions which surrounded His place of birth, we find them not wanting in earnest followers and deep devotion. That a great Messiah was anticipated was no indication that a new religion was anticipated or needed, or that any radical changes were believed necessary. In fact, it was because Jesus announced very early in His mission that He did not agree with and could not support all of the ideas embodied in the Jewish faith that He attracted antagonism toward Himself and made most of the Jews feel that He could not be the anticipated Messiah.

THE SECRET DOCTRINES OF JESUS

Only once before in the history of civilization had there come to earth a spiritual leader and guide whose teachings and practices were so radically different, and whose first steps were to tear down the established religious beliefs of the times. That one great light was the Egyptian Pharaoh, Amenhotep IV, who later became known as Akhenaten and who directed the spiritual meditations of man away from the multiplicity of symbolical gods to the "sole ever-living God."

And so we find that Jesus came into the midst of a comparatively new country where a new religion, or a revision of the existing religion, seemed to be the least needed, and from the very start spoke as a modernist of the purest water. What, then, can we say about the life mission of this greatest of all modernists? We find the answer symbolized in one of His own statements where He said that He came as a messenger of God to be the redeemer and Saviour of man. He did not come with a sword to destroy life, but with a fiery sword to destroy evil and to give truth more power. He came to see that the laws revealed to man in all the ages past were no longer to be ignored and abrogated at will, or denied, but to be obeyed and fulfilled.

THE SECRET DOCTRINES OF JESUS

But He did have a secret mission which He explained in detail to His secret students in His secret school. That mission, we will find in later chapters, was to suffer vicariously for the sins of all men, vicariously to purge them of all evil, even of the original sin inherited by all mankind, and to suffer and sacrifice His earthly appointment and divinity that they might receive the Holy Ghost and establish on earth the Kingdom of Heaven.

What a marvelous, as well as unique, mission!

Is there any reason to wonder why He enshrouded His mission with mystery and secrecy? Was He not to reveal to man the greatest of all mysteries, and were not these mysteries secret ones? Was not such a mission fraught with dangers and with dire consequences to all political, social, and religious standards and practices throughout the world?

We find in analyzing His mission, and by taking His own words and putting them together to compare with His practices and His private instructions, that in addition to appearing before the public as a Light of Men, as another John the Baptist, or another Amenhotep, or another leader of spiritual unfoldment, preaching openly and to all mankind publicly, He was to lay the foundation—the strange, mysterious foundation—

THE SECRET DOCTRINES OF JESUS

for that invisible superstructure which was to constitute the miracle of all miracles, the "Atonement" for men's sins and the washing of their souls in the "Blood of the Lamb."

Throughout the ages the lamb had been the symbol of a great mystery, and its blood had been spared for special sacrifice at times and places in cycles of unfolding civilization when the populace had never realized the spiritual or mystical significance of the ceremony, and it had remained the mystery of all mysteries unrevealed even to the greatest Lights that had hinted at its significance. Jesus, as part of His great mission, was not to continue to mystify His followers with the symbol of the lamb, or with reference to its blood, or with further reference to the possibility of man's complete redemption and purification, but to actually demonstrate the mystery, rend the veil asunder, and expose to the soul of all mankind the process of purification and the Way to salvation.

Such a tremendous mission had to be carried out in its earliest stages with the greatest degree of secrecy and care. A premature revelation of the facts, an untimely discovery of His plans, a profane application of His mystical principles, would have made His mission harder, would have frustrated many of His fondest hopes and desires, and more serious than this, would have prevented the ultimate and final demonstration of the proof of His teachings by which the faith of the world was drawn to Him and His teachings, and the "rock" of His church firmly placed in the proper cycles of human evolution.

So we find that the divine appointment, preordination, birth, and earthly preparation of this greatest of all leaders of men occurred in just that cycle of human history, in just that period of human unfoldment and development, in just that place, and in just the right conditions where the greatest good could be accomplished. The realization of this alone should warrant every Christian—every analytical thinker—in believing that Jesus was uniquely conceived and born to fill a *unique* mission, and to make manifest to the world the secret mystery—the mystery of all mysteries.

▽

Chapter V

THE STEWARDSHIP AND DISCIPLESHIP OF THE CHRISTIAN MYSTERIES

▽

HE average devout Christian will be surprised, no doubt, to read that the true Christian doctrines and practices are fraught with real mysteries and that the secret mission of Jesus and His Disciples was to first practice and apply these mysteries and then dispense the secret laws involved in them to the worthy Disciples and thus enable them to carry out their special missions throughout the world. The Christian church of today, with its rituals and modernized doctrines, leaves in the mind of the sincere follower the impression that all of the mysteries of Christianity pertain to the sacraments and features of the ritual and do not deal with natural law or divine laws applicable to natural and practical affairs of life.

From a careful cross-questioning of the understanding of thousands of Christians in the past years, I have found that these persons, despite long and careful Bible study and sincere analysis of the Christian principles, have a general idea

THE SECRET DOCTRINES OF JESUS

that whatever mysteries there may have been associated with religious rites and doctrines, were contained in the ancient pagan ideas and teachings, and that these mysteries were dispelled and classified and in most cases made inconsequential and wholly transparent by the revelations given to the world by Jesus. In other words, they seem to think that in the pagan, heathen, primitive and mythological teachings of the people of India, Egypt, Persia, and elsewhere, there were so-called strange and mysterious claims and pretentious demonstrations, often dramatized and presented with impressive and hypnotizing surroundings and called "mysteries" in order to dumbfound and perplex the followers of these rites and blindly lead them on or tempt them into a form of worship which forever kept them in the dark regarding the truth of these so-called mysteries. The persons who hold to this belief logically conclude that the coming of Christianity and the diffusion of new Light by Jesus and His Disciples cleared away these mysteries which were held as facts by the multitudes and freed them from being enslaved to false beliefs and mysterious powers that were not divine or supernatural but magical, and produced, or made manifest, through trickery intended to deceive the gullible.

THE SECRET DOCTRINES OF JESUS

The truth of the matter is that the early Christian doctrines and practices contained more mysteries and more genuine secrets of mysterious laws and principles than were ever known to the pagans. While it is unquestionably true that in the early pagan religions we find many so-called mysteries which are only clever concealments of truth and magical manipulations of natural law, nevertheless, many of them were based upon fundamental truths representing the genuine mysteries of life. The illuminating teachings of Jesus and His Disciples did dispel the trickery in many of the mysteries of the pagans, but Jesus brought new light to bear upon many of these ancient mysteries and thereby developed the mysteries into sublime and transcendental revelations and demonstrations of truth.

The mysteries which Jesus taught His Disciples, and which He and they used in their specific forms of missionary work, were never separated from the Christian church and have never ceased to be an element essential to Christian theology and Christian doctrine. It is true, however, that as the Christian religion became systematized, ritualized and modernized, the transcendental mysteries which Jesus came to earth to reveal, and which constituted the highest spiritual element in His teachings and practices, became *lost* to the outer

THE SECRET DOCTRINES OF JESUS

circle of membership of the early Christian church, and finally unknown even to the most advanced and proficient creators and teachers of the Christian gospels.

It is a question today whether those fathers who constituted the first Fathers of the Holy Roman Church knew anything more of these sublime mysteries than the fact that Jesus had demonstrated them, had revealed them to His first Disciples, and used them in the working of miracles and the performance of His obligations as a teacher and a missionary. It is probably true, however, that in the innermost secret archives of the Holy Roman Church today are preserved the truths of these great mysteries and the laws that make it possible for the highly spiritualized individual to demonstrate them and make them manifest. In fact, some of these mysteries, utilizing natural and divine laws for their manifestation, have been applied in the past centuries by the highest of the ecclesiastical dignitaries of the inner circle of the Holy Roman Church and have been placed at the disposal of many of its cardinals and special workers. Certainly we have a right to assume that the inner circle of the Church, known as the College of Cardinals, is in possession of the wisdom and knowledge relating to these great mysteries and can apply the laws and perform seeming miracles

THE SECRET DOCTRINES OF JESUS

when they find it necessary to do so. If these eminent Fathers of the Christian church are not familiar with these mysteries and the use of them, it is a greater criticism upon them for their lack of such knowledge and their impotent stewardship.

It is clearly pointed out in the slightly veiled, but often plainly stated remarks of the Apostles in the New Testament that the secret doctrines and mysteries, which Jesus came to earth to demonstrate, reveal and teach, constituted a transcendental gift from God to the selected and appointed Apostles who were to consider themselves as stewards of these things and not as the personal recipients of an individual blessing. They were to dispense these truths and these mysteries as stewards and not hold the secret knowledge and wisdom within their own consciousness as a rightful personal possession.

We see in this idea one of the earliest of the mystical principles, fully known and maintained as a fundamental law and practice by the devout followers of various mystical brotherhoods and organizations today. The rare wisdom and divine knowledge that come to the sincere mystic through revelations, or through the study of ancient manuscripts loaned him from the archives of his brotherhood, are not to be absorbed into the consciousness

THE SECRET DOCTRINES OF JESUS

of the student and the adept as intellectual power, or gifts for the purpose of increasing his personal prowess and to serve him selfishly in his mastership of life. He learns from the earliest stage of his mystical development that if he is found worthy to be the recipient of such knowledge and understanding of the mysteries, and develops any degree of capability in applying natural and divine law to the revelation, demonstration, manifestation or use of the mysteries of life, he will do so only as a channel, or an instrument or a servant laboring in the vineyard of mankind and performing his demonstrations and applying his knowledge in behalf of God's and the divine universal Consciousness. Any attempt, therefore, to hold such knowledge secretly within one's own consciousness and fail to dispense it to the worthy, even if it were not used selfishly, would constitute failure to meet the obligations and duties of stewardship; and this is a greater sin than to permit the too frequent use of the knowledge to such an extent that it may occasionally redound to the benefit of the individual acting as an instrument or servant.

We cannot conceive, therefore, of any claim rightly made that explains the absence of the practice and revelation of the mysteries in the Christian church today on the ground that the fathers of the

THE SECRET DOCTRINES OF JESUS

church are either ignorant of these mysteries or prefer to conceal them.

The absence of these mysteries in the teachings and practices of the Christian church today constitutes the basis of the most serious criticism that is made against the church, both Protestant and Roman Catholic. While the average devotee of the Christian religion does not know what the great mysteries were that have been concealed or held in restraint, and may even doubt that there ever were such mysteries, he is becoming more and more familiar with the fact that many cults and sects outside of the orthodox Christian churches are using what they call divine laws and principles and Christian mysteries with which to perform these seeming miracles and to carry on practices in behalf of humanity that simulate the practices of the early Christian Disciples. That these cults can use a wisdom or knowledge which they call mystical or metaphysical, divine or Christian, and perform extraordinary demonstrations of healing and of mastership in the affairs of life, has not only caused a heavy drain upon the membership of the orthodox Christian churches and weakened their ranks of fellowship, but it also has led analytical minds to suspect at least that there was wisdom, knowledge and power, known to Jesus

THE SECRET DOCTRINES OF JESUS

and His Disciples and probably to the early church fathers, that is not included in the Christian church of today nor used by Christian workers as a part of their Christian duties.

This unfortunate condition of affairs—which has caused many schisms in the Christian church and brought about a large membership in the combined mystical and metaphysical cults and societies of today—has been considered as deplorable by many of the leading Christian theologians in the past century. Many of them have pointed out that the absence of the mystical features, the genuine mysteries and the divine practices in the Christian churches of today, constitutes the real reason for the slow growth and the heavy withdrawal of members in all of the Christian denominations.

While clergymen of all denominations have expressed themselves quite frequently regarding the influence that these multitudinous sects, cults, and secret schools have had in the growth and development of the Christian church, and have pointed out that these new movements constitute a serious form of rivalry to the Christian church, they fail to realize that the fault lies within their own church and that if the Christian church of today would awaken and quicken the spirit of the Christian mysteries and practices that Jesus taught His

THE SECRET DOCTRINES OF JESUS

Disciples, and which they used in all of their missionary work, the rival movements and systems would have no excuse for their existence and would, in fact, cease to exist because of the immediate return to the Christian fold of millions who have become either indifferent or absolutely discouraged.

One of the greatest of modern theologians and spiritual analysts was the late Dr. Robert Norwood, one time pastor of a rapidly growing church in Philadelphia and later chosen to be the great Light of the Church of St. Bartholomew in New York. At one conclave of Episcopal churchmen assembled to discuss matters of the church and solve its more immediate problems, Dr. Norwood contended that "the greatest need of the Christian church today is to return to the mystical teachings and mystery revelations of the genuine Christian foundation."

That the Disciples of Jesus knew that they were dealing with the mysteries which were secret and doctrines which were new and therefore unrevealed, is found in all of their utterances recorded in their writings in the New Testament. One needs only to note such statements on the part of Jesus and the Disciples as these:

THE SECRET DOCTRINES OF JESUS

"It is given unto you to know the mysteries; unto you it is given to know the mysteries; we speak the wisdom of God in a mystery; and we are the stewards of the mysteries of God and understand all the mysteries; having made known unto us the mysteries; and being of the fellowship of the mysteries, we make known the mysteries of the gospels and the mystery which hath been hid from ages; holding the mystery of the faith in pureness," etc. These phrases and many more like them will be found in: Matthew 13:11, Mark 4:11, Luke 8:10, Romans 11:25, 16:25, I Corinthians 2:7, 4:1, 13:2, 14:2, 15:51, Ephesians 1:9, 3:3, 3:4, 3:9, 5:32, Colossians 1:26, 1:27, 2:2, 4:3, II Thessalonians 2:7, I Timothy 3:9, 3:16, Revelation 1:20, 10:7, 17:5, 17:7.

Now, in the very beginning of our discussion of this matter, let us have a correct understanding regarding what is meant by the words "mystery" and "mysteries" as used by Jesus and the Apostles in the Gospels of the New Testament. It must not be believed that the word "mystery" referred to any unusual or uncommon or extraordinary occurrence or principle which upon simple explanation ceased to be either a mystery or a law difficult to understand. One of the most eminent of authorities in the analysis of words and terms used by

THE SECRET DOCTRINES OF JESUS

the writers of the books of the Bible was Robert Young whose analytical concordance to the Bible, published in 1893, is still an unequalled source of reliable information in these matters. He states that the word "mystery" as used in the New Testament by the writers of the Gospels meant 'that which is known only to the initiated."

Another source of reliable information on this point is that excellent commentary and book of critical and explanatory terms written and edited by Rev. Robert Jamison of St. Paul's Church, Glasgow, Scotland; the Rev. A. R. Fausset of St. Cuthbert's, York, England; and the Rev. David Brown, Professor of Theology of Aberdeen, Scotland. In their exhaustive comments regarding the use of the terms "mystery" and "mysteries" by Jesus and His Disciples they tell us, "The word 'mysteries' in scripture is not used in its classical sense of religious secrets, nor yet of things incomprehensible or in their own nature difficult to be understood—but in the sense of things of purely divine revelation, and usually things darkly announced under the ancient economy, and during all that period darkly understood, but fully published under the gospel. . . . The 'mysteries of the Kingdom of Heaven,' then, mean those glorious gospel truths which at that time only the more

THE SECRET DOCTRINES OF JESUS

advanced Disciples could appreciate and that but partially."

From the explanation given by the first authority, in which explanation the word "initiated" is used, and from the explanation given by the latter authorities, in which the term "more advanced Disciples" is used, we find that these writers evidently discerned the great truth that was represented by the word *mystery*.

The mysteries which Jesus taught His Disciples, and which they held in such great secrecy and which they studied diligently to make manifest and to demonstrate and to apply and use in their missionary work, constituted supernatural or transcendental revelations and operations of law that only the initiated or the more advanced Disciples were permitted to understand or to apply. We shall see in later chapters that these Disciples of Jesus —the one hundred and twenty of them constituting His secret school—were initiates, for they had an initiation ceremony and they had secret means of identifying themselves such as passwords, signs and tokens. They were the more advanced of the thousands of followers of Jesus, representing those who had pledged their very lives in support of His work, and each of whom had been given a special mission—in contradistinction to the other followers who were merely casual listeners, most of them selfishly seeking relief from physical suffering or hoping to aggrandize themselves by their association with a new movement and a surprising and startling system of thought. In the ancient pagan schools and mystical or mythological systems of secret study it had become a general practice to refer to their secret mysteries by symbols or tokens and to speak of the secret teachings in parables lest the uninitiated populace might discover the secret truths.

When the child Jesus was taken into Egypt by His parents, He was too young to realize that He was entering a land where nearly all of the great truths of life were carved on stones or painted on walls in symbols or allegorical designs which revealed great principles in parables. But as His youthful education was developed to a point where He was able, in His thirteenth year, to astonish the Elders of His country, He came to learn that the only safe way of preserving truths, and of conveying them to the worthy and withholding them from the selfish and unworthy, was to write them in symbols and to speak of them in parables and allegories. We should not be surprised to find, therefore, that with the greatest of all mysteries having been revealed to Him, and with the greatest of

THE SECRET DOCTRINES OF JESUS

divine wisdom conveyed to His consciousness by God that He might be a messenger to dispense these truths, He quickly adopted the system of speaking in parables and allegories, and adopted signs and symbols in order to conceal from the uninitiated what only the initiated and duly qualified workers should understand in all detail.

Some of the most ancient of the mystery symbols and secret signs used in allegorical and mystical writings and teachings were the triangle, the cross, the circle, the square, and their components —such as a straight vertical line, a straight horizontal line, a diagonal line, and a curved line. Jesus did not arbitrarily adopt these ancient symbols in connection with His system of secret communication of knowledge or in the presentation of parables and allegories, nor did He adopt them merely because He found them conveniently at hand. He adopted them because each of them represented a fundamental sublime truth that had been revealed by God to the great Lights of the past ages in their primitive and preliminary program of enlightening mankind, and Jesus knew that the great truths which they symbolized were still the great truths of life and meant something to the initiated mind, the inspired or attuned mind, but meant nothing at all to the unworthy, the

THE SECRET DOCTRINES OF JESUS

unthinking, and the undeveloped. And so we find Jesus using these ancient symbols in the same way in which they had been used for ages to represent a fundamental truth. But, in the light of the new revelations and the new mysteries He was to give to His Disciples, these symbols—and allegories in which they were interwoven to make a seemingly understandable story—took on a new light, a new power of reaching the soul and the mind. That is why we find in the books of the New Testament so many references by the Disciples to the fact that Jesus "spake many things unto them in parables."

Speaking of these parables, the same eminent authorities whom we have already quoted, state in their book that "these parables are seven in number; and it is not a little remarkable that while this is the *sacred* number, the first four of them were spoken to the mixed multitudes, while the remaining three were spoken to the twelve in private —these divisions, four and three, being themselves notable in the symbolic arithmetic of Scripture." Here we see reference to the fact that in the mysteries, as revealed by Jesus to His Disciples, there was a continuation of the use of the seven sacred numbers that had been used in the ancient mysteries and that seven was considered by Jesus and

THE SECRET DOCTRINES OF JESUS

His Disciples, as *the* sacred number, and not *a* sacred number, just as it is today among those mystical brotherhoods which are attempting to preserve and perpetuate for all time the genuine mysteries and secret doctrines of Christianity. We see, furthermore, how easily these numbers of one to seven constitute the first section of the symbols already referred to, 1 representing one of the straight lines, 2 representing two lines, 3 representing the triangle, and 4 the square. And we note that these authors used the term "symbolic arithmetic of Scripture."

As we read in detail of the teachings and preachings of Jesus when surrounded by some of His Disciples, or only a few, or in the midst of the multitudes, we find that He used parables except when He spoke alone in the secrecy and privacy of His school of one hundred and twenty initiated and qualified students. As He went up and down the highways of Palestine and found a convenient mound or rock upon which He could stand and look over the assembly of individuals who would gradually gather together along the stony roads, or attract the attention of those who were passing rapidly by on their donkeys, He quite often found it necessary to deliver His message and to drive home His brief sermon in a story which instantly

THE SECRET DOCTRINES OF JESUS

interested the passers-by because it dealt with their personal problems, and with things which were familiar to them and not abstract and speculative.

He was always accompanied by one or two of His Disciples—especially the twelve Apostles who represented a sort of bodyguard and innermost circle or executive committee, as we might name it today—and in every community there were one or two of His secret school who would stand in the middle or on the outskirts of the increasing circle of listeners, ready to benefit by the demonstrations that Jesus would make of proper poise and attitude in preaching, the proper spiritual vibrations to send forth that the hearers might be impressed with His spiritual love and honest concern for their best interests. And we can easily visualize motley crowds with their multi-colored robes, sashes, and headdresses, many of them very, very poor, a few very wealthy, most of them of the middle working class. Nearly all of them were educated to some degree, especially in the doctrines of their religion which made them familiar with certain theological terms and terminology, and many of them were ready to scoff and laugh and ridicule any idea or any thought that appeared to be contrary to their religious convictions, just as we find the multitude today.

THE SECRET DOCTRINES OF JESUS

And so He would talk to this motley crowd in parables, first choosing for the very opening sentences a key word or two that would attract their vacillating attention and make His suggestions seem appealing and familiar to them. He did not talk over their heads nor did He talk down to them, for He created even in the minds of the great and learned the impression that He was unusually brilliant of mind. If He had attempted to talk down to the intelligence of the average individual in the crowd before Him, He would have created the impression of being loosely educated and poorly qualified to hold the attention of any group of individuals. But He had that magic ability, undoubtedly divinely inspired but very carefully trained and developed, of inventing parables which dealt with their immediate worldly problems. Some of the parables dealt with the problems of those who lived in distant lands, and we can plainly see by these that some time during His youth—and prior to the beginning of His worldly ministry— He must have lived and studied in these other lands among the people to whom He referred and of whose problems He gave such detailed and accurate pictures. When He spoke at places where the men—and the women—were mostly concerned with fishing, His parables dealt with stories and

THE SECRET DOCTRINES OF JESUS

incidents of those who were fishermen. When He spoke to those whose daily industry and labor was associated with the making of wine, He used a parable that involved the principles of wine making.

When we recall that the language He used also fitted the quality and intellectual understanding and nationality of His people, such as the Jewish language when talking to the Jews, and the Aramaic language when talking to the Gentiles and others, we see that He used every means which would aid Him in symbolically and allegorically conveying the truths that would help them without placing in their hands the secret truths and doctrines which they would misuse, misapply, and probably never comprehend in the right manner. With His hands He would make certain signs, which would appear to the passer-by as mere gestures to accompany His oratory, but which would appear to His initiated students as signs revealing symbolical truths. In the parables were words and phrases which had dual meanings. The word *wine* meant a commercial product to the grape growers and wine makers, but to the initiated it had the meaning which it always had in the mysteries and in the sacred teachings of the spiritual side of man. When He spoke of the fisherman and referred to the nets, and the tears in them which had to be repaired, He conveyed two different ideas to the two classes of listeners—the initiated, and the uninitiated.

Unfortunately, in the translation of the writings of the Apostles, many mistakes have been made by the translators in modern times, they being unfamiliar with the current or possibly the vernacular meanings of some of the words used in this ancient period. For this reason there are certain secret and mystical references in His parables which are not readily discerned by even the most profound of the church fathers and preachers. Again, some of the words which He used in the Aramaic language had a slightly different meaning from a similar word in the Jewish language. An excellent example of this is shown in His allegorical statement about it being more difficult for a rich man to enter the Kingdom of God than for a camel to enter the eye of a needle. That symbolical or allegorical statement has always been a puzzle to students of allegory or metaphor. What relationship could there possibly be between a camel and the eye of a needle? Even a child would wonder at such a reference, since it did not relate to any problem or difficulty ever experienced by the ones to whom He was preaching.

THE SECRET DOCTRINES OF JESUS

When we stop to think of the fact that this allegorical statement was made to men and women in the fishing industry, and when we stop further to realize that one of their problems was the daily repair of torn nets, and that one of their great hopes was to find a strong cord which would yet be small enough to go through the eye of the needle which they used in repairing nets, we can understand that this particular metaphor was intended to make a great impression upon the fishermen and their wives who attended to the repair of the nets.

But still, the reference to a "camel" is inconsistent.

In the Aramaic language which He used we find, through careful translation, that the Aramaic word could be interpreted in one form of conversation as *camel*, while among fishermen the word meant *rope*. Therefore, what Jesus said to these people who were puzzled with the problem of finding a large strong rope that would go through the needle in mending the nets, was that it is more difficult for a rich man to enter the Kingdom of God than for a rope to go through the eye of a needle. The word *rope* conveyed to them the idea of a large, heavy, twisted piece of hemp many times larger than the needle itself and, therefore, the metaphor was a personal one to be used safely, whereas the reference to the "camel" going through the eye of the needle meant absolutely nothing to them.

All of the parables contained very pointed references and secret words and terms which made the allegory and the parable fraught with the most vital truths of the great mysteries; and if a hearer was one of those extraordinary persons whom Jesus hoped to find from time to time, and who with eyes could see and with ears could hear, then He would have won one more convert, or at least started one more thinking mind upon the right path.

Even His allegory regarding the casting of the seeds to the ground, and the manner in which some fell by the wayside on stones while some fell into good ground and grew and took root, represented the problem He confronted in speaking to the populace.

But in the future chapters we shall see that all of the principles developed in His church in connection with the rituals and the sacraments, and as the foundation of His Christian ideals and practices, were based upon secrets that still have a mystical meaning, a secret interpretation, and a sublime, transcendental application little known or

THE SECRET DOCTRINES OF JESUS

suspected by the average Christian follower and unincorporated in the system of Christian instruction adopted by the modern Christian churches.

▽

Chapter VI
INDIVIDUAL SECRET MISSIONS
▽

AS WE study and carefully analyze the activities of the Disciples and the Apostles and the members of the great secret school formed by Jesus, we find that while each of them was pledged to give his life in fulfilling a great mission, and each was given a special "authority and power," the mission assigned was not the same in every case.

The mission of Jesus was unquestionably the most complex and the most burdensome that could be assigned to a human being, and at the very beginning Jesus must have foreseen and realized that the complexity of His mission, its diversity of action, its many responsibilities, and most of all the continued placing of Himself in the center of the limelight, would bring the direst of punishment following the most severe criticisms. Never in the history of the development of civilization had one man so willingly assumed such a great mission in life. Jesus *assumed* it although it was preordained. He knew that He could not refuse; therefore, He did not, because it was His divine duty, and the only reason for the Word of God to be made flesh and for His soul and consciousness to be made incarnate on earth. We cannot imagine—with all of our human capabilities of inventing and imagining every possible event of human action—what would have occurred in the process of earthly civilization and the advancement of man's spiritual growth on earth if Jesus, upon reaching manhood and realizing what was before Him, had refused to participate in that ceremony of Baptism in the River Jordan when the Holy Ghost descended upon Him and He became the Saviour of Man, the Redeemer, and the one to bear all of the sins of man and to be sacrificed for man's salvation.

But we find that in carrying out the work of His school He did not put upon the shoulders or into the consciousness of any one of His Disciples or Apostles all of the responsibilities, all of the details of the mission that He Himself had assumed. He probably realized that no one human individual outside of Himself, uniquely and divinely born for it, could assume such a position in life. But He also probably realized that the greatest efficiency, the greatest results, and the most perfect realization of the steps toward bringing the Kingdom of Heaven on earth, would be fulfilled after His crucifixion by dividing His own responsibilities, His

THE SECRET DOCTRINES OF JESUS

own features of missionary work, and His own efforts, among the hundred and twenty and making each Disciple or worker a specialist in one or two particular requirements or necessities.

It appears, therefore, that He divided His own program of earthly activities into twelve sections and selected ten of the Disciples and students for each of these twelve classifications. In other words, in each classification of specialized activities there would be precisely ten men or women. This would give Him the round number of a hundred and twenty workers. At the head of each classification He placed one of the Apostles as chairman, let us say, or chief advisor. This gave Him the twelve special Apostles who constituted also His immediate consultation board or group of advisors and intimates.

Some of these workers were sent afield and into foreign countries early in the great scheme, for the work they had to do did not require the same length of preparation and study in the secret school that was necessary for others. Some of these hundred and twenty workers were forever to remain unknown as special parts of His great plan. In fact, some of them were sworn to such absolute secrecy and to such a secrecy of detail that they were never to be seen close to Him throughout

THE SECRET DOCTRINES OF JESUS

His entire ministry, were never to be seen taking any particular interest in any discussions or demonstrations along the highways or in the byways and never to be seen talking with the other Disciples or workers concerning anything more than a very casual comment about business or daily affairs. None of them was ever to wear any special robes, except robes that would indicate that they belonged perhaps to one or more of the very many cults existing in that day and which had moral, ethical, spiritual, or cultural reform for their seeming purpose.

It was not uncommon for the average person in Palestine and Syria of that time to be known as a member of some class or sect or group—perhaps of a spiritual, social or business nature—and that is not unusual even today. If we went carefully through one of the largest office buildings in any large American city today, and received complete answers to our questions, we would find that one businessman belongs to the Rotarians, another to the Kiwanis Club, another to the Chamber of Commerce, another to the Junior Chamber of Commerce, and another to the High Twelve and another to the Low Twelve, and to this or that, including the mystical organizations such as the Rosicrucians. In fact, one of the problems that

THE SECRET DOCTRINES OF JESUS

confronted Jesus was the analysis of these various cults and organizations early in His years of preparation. He had to know, first of all, what each one of the sects or cults represented or claimed to advocate. Then He had to become familiar with some of their secret ways of working, their secret means of identification, and any secret or ulterior motives or plans they might have in mind. We find Jesus making many references to this multiplicity of personal, private, secret interests and He had to pass this information on to His Disciples.

On the other hand, many of His Apostles, Disciples and workers were not sworn to such secrecy —except perhaps as to the real mission they had in mind. But they could meet with Him or be seen talking with Him or joining the ranks of His other followers in any great open-air meeting or any performance of a miracle.

Some of the secret details of these private missions are very interesting and we shall touch upon them in the chapters of this book dealing with the secret doctrines. Some of the Disciples were sworn to labor solely among the despondent and hopeless. Others had to work among the so-called radicals or those who were ready to tear down and destroy the good institutions of the day along with the evil ones, fired solely with the desire of accomplish-

THE SECRET DOCTRINES OF JESUS

ing something heroic. Others had to work among the hypocrites of the synagogue, who were deliberately spreading false ideas about the devout with the hope of personally benefiting by any reactions that might result. There were others who had to spend much time making the acquaintance of Roman officials, and of the Jewish rulers or those in positions to serve the Roman officials, in order that these important personages might be kept properly informed in casual conversation of what was going on.

If we carefully read between the lines of the most crucial days and weeks in the life of Jesus, we find that always someone informed Roman officials of what was going on here, there, and elsewhere. At first one gets the impression that a number of spies within the group of Apostles and Disciples were deliberately informing Roman and Jewish officials about the work of Jesus in order that they might persecute Him as well as prosecute Him. But as one goes on in the study of these events, and notes the direct good that came from many of these situations, it appears to have been a systematic plan of informing the higher officials in a manner that made it unnecessary for them to send forth unreliable investigators or those who might have returned the wrong information.

THE SECRET DOCTRINES OF JESUS

The whole scheme was far more complex than the Christian churches of today present it to us. But the complexity was due almost wholly to the fact that the secret doctrines which Jesus wanted to teach and demonstrate—and then establish in the lives of men—were so simple, so childlike in their fundamental nature and so easily applied if properly understood, that a more complex system of presenting the instruction was necessary than in a case where the reverse would have been true. In other words, one of the important things that Jesus had to establish in the minds of the people was *faith*. He tried to impress upon them on many occasions that faith was responsible for all that He accomplished and that if they had faith they could even move mountains. Such faith as this they had never known. It was a childlike faith, like that of the child who believes that his parents are capable of any accomplishment because they are so great and so wonderful.

But, to establish such faith as this, it was necessary to establish a very complex system that would continually keep the simplicity of matters before the public; otherwise analysis and discussion of the principles on the part of the ignorant would have led into dialectical dissertations and philosophical

THE SECRET DOCTRINES OF JESUS

forums in which all the simplicity of the doctrines of Jesus would have been lost.

When Jesus tried to tell those who were following Him, and who stopped to watch the woman kiss His garment, that her *faith* alone was responsible for the reaction from this kiss, He was face to face with one of the most difficult psychological problems known to man.

One inherent primitive tendency which is born in all of us is to want to attribute the unusual to the supernatural, and this tendency is so strong that there are persons living today who would look upon the striking of a match on the side of a match box, thus producing a flame, not as a simple scientific demonstration, but a supernatural thing, a miracle of miracles. And the strange thing is that these persons would rather believe it was supernatural than scientific, and they would prefer and seek and demand the complex, hypothetical explanation that involved all of the supernatural beliefs of the past instead of accepting the simple facts. So in order to understand the secret doctrines as Jesus taught them to His Disciples, and as they were truly put forth in the activities of the early Christian church, we shall proceed to analyze first His school and the manner in which the students met or came together,

THE SECRET DOCTRINES OF JESUS

and then analyze the doctrines as they were taught and applied by the different Apostles and Disciples.

▽

Chapter VII
STRANGE BIBLICAL PASSAGES

▽

WE CAN find the whole story of the secret mission of Jesus, the secret school, His secret Disciples and their secret activities, in the Gospels of the New Testament. Many innocent looking verses and paragraphs in these Books have been passed over very lightly and inconsiderately by thousands of Biblical students. They have been read and quoted, and even partly analyzed, by Christian clergymen of all denominations the world over. On the other hand, thousands of sincere Christians have been puzzled by the strange ideas expressed in some of those verses and have even suspected them of having a hidden meaning.

In all of my researches I have found but one or two outstanding theologians or experts of Biblical interpretation who have attempted to unveil or separate the suspected double meanings or hidden meanings. I have heard some clergymen say, in using some of these verses as texts and in attempting to explain them, that there was probably another meaning to be found, but it did not seem

THE SECRET DOCTRINES OF JESUS

to be "God's will at this time to make it plain to man." But, it is from these very verses and paragraphs, sprinkled profusely, consistently, and deliberately throughout the Books of the New Testament, that we derive a good picture of the origin, nature, and activities of the secret school of divine wisdom conducted by Jesus, and His secret methods of presenting His secret doctrines.

It is my intention to give to the reader at this moment a picture of one incident of the history and activities of this secret school. I have chosen a very propitious time in the life of Jesus and the history of His school. I have selected the occasion of the most important of all of the secret school sessions, the one when He was to confer upon His Graduates the Divine Diploma and certificate of authority as the culmination of His process of conferring upon them the knowledge and power to carry on their individual missions.

The occasion was just a day or two after Jesus had probably reached the very peak of His antagonism toward the hypocritical traditions and practices of some of the leaders of the Jewish faith. He had come into the temple and chased the money-changers from it and thereby purified it—and at the same time made an enemy of one of the leading Lights of the synagogue who de-

THE SECRET DOCTRINES OF JESUS

rived a personal income from the profits of the questionable practices involved in the changing of money. He had caused the Jews and the Romans alike to say, "It is high time we go after this fellow and break him and put him in his proper place!" And it was also just a few hours before the time set for His betrayal and the inevitable Crucifixion.

Let no one think for a moment that Jesus was suddenly surprised or unexpectedly shocked by either the act of Judas in betraying Him or the secret plans that were being made for His public disgrace after a manifestly illegal trial. For weeks and months the legal Lights who could be induced or bribed into lending their assistance had been preparing the papers for such a trial as Rome had never heard of before, and such as the Jews never hoped to witness again. No doubt the cross was being made secretly and all the devices of torture were being prepared. The whole procedure that seemed to come as the sudden, stupendous climax of His life was a well-evolved drama, plotted weeks, months, years, and even centuries before in the evil consciousness of that portion of all human nature which abhors the presentation of truth, the coming of Light, the dispelling of Darkness, and the victory of Spirituality. Jesus knew in His

THE SECRET DOCTRINES OF JESUS

youth, during the earliest days of His preparation for the future ministry, that it would end just as it did end. But He also knew that in a certain number of years, months, weeks, days, and hours He must accomplish the great mission of His life and not permit the grand climax to come upon Him before He was ready.

So, on this particular night, while He was living in Bethany and still thundering His message and His challenge during the day, He arranged to have the final and ultimate worldly assembly of the Apostles who constituted the Advisory Council of His secret school. He had held forth as a promise to them certain rich rewards for their studies and their practices, for their faith and their loyalty, and as a fulfillment of their ambitions to carry on their missions. He had promised them, as the richest of rewards, the transference from on high to each of them individually of the necessary power and authority to carry on the work He had carried on, and do even greater things. Throughout the years in which His secret school functioned, He had consistently and perfectly adhered to a definite curriculum, a definite course of study which included private, secret lectures, private demonstrations in their secret meeting places and in carefully selected open spaces in the countryside, with personal demonstrations on His own part on various occasions when complex conditions surrounded Him, so that they would be accustomed to meeting and overcoming the antagonistic attitudes and interferences of the multitudes in their own missionary activities.

He recalled the beginning of His campaign when He opened His first public announcements from a hilltop near the Sea of Galilee and just outside of Capernaum. Those first talks were properly designed to attract the attention of the thinking minds and of those adherents of the Galilean doctrines who were looking for something more than a mere figurehead of the church as a Messiah, but for one coming with great wisdom. While He wanted His truths to reach the poor and the ignorant and to do them much good, He sought at the same time to make another appeal to the intellectual, to the powerful, that they might be drawn unto Him and thereby show the others that here was not merely a message of appeasement for the poor or a message of hope for the sick, or a message of consolation to the dying, nor even a bit of encouragement to the hypocritical of the faith.

As He journeyed around the Sea of Galilee, and down through the old familiar districts and then farther south toward Jerusalem, He studied and analyzed the crowds who gathered around Him.

THE SECRET DOCTRINES OF JESUS

After many weeks He was able to pick out a few here and there whom He recognized as constant followers. Some had started to follow Him at Capernaum, some had joined Him at Tiberias; some appeared for the first time at His gatherings at the place now called Nazareth, and near Mary's well. He recognized a few who had come from Nabulus and who were of the Samaritans and who presented every sign and indication of intelligence and spiritual insight. To these consistent followers, who were sacrificing much of their time and their comfort and even much of their material affairs to hear Him speak often and to be close to Him, He offered a special meeting on one occasion and secretly told them that He would like to talk to them more privately and make them personal students if they would take up a share of responsibility and a part of the burden of His mission. And gradually, without revealing all of the facts, He bound a number of them to Himself in secrecy and with all of the devotion and love that He hoped to find. It was after His many visits to Jerusalem and to the places in the south that He finally completed His mystical number of a hundred and twenty, or twelve units of ten each, to form the universal circle of discipleship; and now —many years later—He was to give to the leaders

THE SECRET DOCTRINES OF JESUS

of these faithful students and loyal friends the last words of instruction, and witness their ordination and spiritual Baptism, with the final command to *go forth!*

These students had learned by this time, as had the multitudes and as had the critical representatives of the Jewish faith who had listened to His teachings and carefully watched His demonstrations, that Jesus spoke with a *power* and an *authority* that no preacher had ever used before. John the Baptist had performed many wonderful manifestations of divine power, but he never convinced his witnesses of the source and nature of that power as had Jesus in a few years. Jesus did not implore; He did not beg of them that for their own sake they should follow His advice. He did not merely point out to them a Path that would lead to the establishment of a new kingdom or take them on their journey through life to the highest goal of their spiritual ambitions. He came to change their ways and said it in a manner that convinced most of them that He might even go so far as to force them to obey and make it necessary for them to do so by the performance of greater miracles than the raising of the dead or the curing of the sick. He might even cause their temples to topple down upon them; He might even cause the rivers to dry

THE SECRET DOCTRINES OF JESUS

and the lakes to become shallow and the winds and rains to storm upon the land.

His students, as well as the multitudes, had come to believe the power which Jesus exercised was an unusually divine power from an unusual source beyond their comprehension. But His pupils also understood in their faith and in their devotion that that miraculous, divine power and authority possessed by Jesus could be bestowed upon them. So the Apostles looked forward to this one great, final session of their official activities as the advisory council in His secret school.

On this particular day, in the very hours of the Jewish Passover and while the whole officialdom was wildly discussing His brazen and bold acts— such as chasing the money-changers out of the temple and making strange prophecies about destroying the temple and building it again—His Apostles contacted one another and went to the secret place where Jesus rested in the evening, and asked Him where they were to go for this important meeting and what they were to do.

From week to week, evidently, they had met at different places or at least had changed their secret meeting place often enough to keep it from the knowledge of the officials and the enemies, and never proceeded to any one of their meetings with-

THE SECRET DOCTRINES OF JESUS

out first learning just where they were to go and how to approach in order not to attract attention and make the place unsafe. And so on this occasion we find that Peter and John met Jesus and He told them to go and notify the others and be prepared for the Passover which they would celebrate quite differently from that being held by the populace. The facts given here are taken from the 22nd chapter of the Book of Luke and from similar passages in the Books of Mark, Matthew, and John.

When Peter and John asked Jesus how they should prepare for this unusual occasion and its unique Passover and where they would find the secret meeting place, Jesus told them to enter the city of Jerusalem, one or two at a time, and proceed down the main street as heretofore, watching for a man who would approach them bearing a pitcher of water. As he approached them and turned on his heel and moved off into another direction, they were to follow him.

It would seem from other citations that at times the secret students of the school would watch for a man whose left foot was unshod, presenting a strange appearance, or whose garment was so arranged that his left knee and lower limb were bare, or whose garment was so torn that his left breast

THE SECRET DOCTRINES OF JESUS

appeared bare. In each instance the peculiar dress, condition or action of the important guide was not only uncommon but significant in accordance with ancient symbology relating to characters of the old secret schools.

On this occasion they were to follow the man carrying the pitcher of water and observe to which doorway he went, pausing, before he returned to the main street. They were to go to this doorway and give a symbolical knock and when the door was opened to them each was to say to the keeper of the door, "Our Teacher has told us to say, 'Where is the guest chamber that we may eat the Passover?'" Jesus explained to them that this keeper of the door would allow them to enter, after hearing their question which would identify them, and he would take them to a large assembly room that was completely furnished and ready for this special ceremony.

The twelve Apostles went in ones and twos in accordance with this secret method and were allowed to enter. If the keeper of the door had refused to allow them to enter, as must have occurred on one or two previous occasions, they would have known that some spy or inspector or representative of the enemy or of the Roman authorities had been

THE SECRET DOCTRINES OF JESUS

prying around and had made the place unsafe for their meeting.

And so on this occasion the twelve Apostles awaited the coming of Jesus, and finally He joined them and announced that He had been looking forward earnestly to this meeting, hoping that everything would work out well and allow them to come together and complete the culmination of His great secret work before His personal suffering and imprisonment and probable crucifixion occurred. Rising, He made the preliminary announcement that the occasion had much to do with the fulfillment of His plans for the establishment of the Kingdom of God on earth.

Then Jesus filled a large cup with wine and drank of it and passed it among the Apostles and told them to divide it among themselves, each taking a drink. Then He explained the symbolism of His prayer and of the division of the wine by telling them that He would not drink of the fruit of the vine again among them or in any other manner until the Kingdom of God had become established. They recognized, in this drinking mutually from the one holy cup, a very old secret symbol of ordination and benediction, and also a symbol of equal power and position in whatever work or mission was signalized by the occasion.

And then Jesus took some of the bread and offered another prayer and invocation asking God's special blessing upon it and then broke it into small pieces and gave a piece to each of them, explaining, "This material form which I now serve to you is symbolical of my body which I give unto you and divide among you, and by it you will serve to remember me as being divided among you and one with you and one of you."

And finally He lifted the great holy cup to His lips again and explained this was the cup of the new covenant and that it contained symbolically His blood which was to be shed for them and through them for the salvation and redemption of the sinners of the world.

The drinking of the wine from the holy cup or grail is still a sacred, symbolical ceremony among the secret schools of the Orient and the Near East and even among some schools of spiritual and sacred wisdom in the Western world. This process of breaking bread and drinking wine was not an original idea with Jesus but a very old and sacred idea which He applied in a new manner because His whole mission on earth was a new mission based upon the ancient sacred symbols and ceremonies. To eat of the bread in this manner was to share the physical body of the Christ, and to

THE SECRET DOCTRINES OF JESUS

drink of the wine was to drink of His blood and thus be not only in holy communion with Him, but a part of Him in whatever sacred work He assigned to them and transferred to them.

It was on this occasion of His last worldly supper with them that He revealed to them again why He had been anxious for many days to have this special ceremony occur. So He proceeded to explain to them that while the officials of the country were seeking Him and trying to find His hiding place to arrest Him and falsely condemn and crucify Him, it would not be until the morning or very late that evening that one of His own supposedly loyal Apostles would betray Him.

Most of His Apostles knew also of the threats that had been made and the danger that surrounded Him and so they were not surprised at His announcement, but they were startled when He told them that one of those sitting right at the very table with Him now, and participating in this last great ceremony, would be the one to betray Him. They were so startled that they began to question Jesus as to whom it could possibly be, and they grew excited and claimed that each of them was the greatest in sincerity and loyalty or that each of them was the chosen Disciple to represent the great work in the future and therefore could not be guilty of such a crime as this. In their desire to establish their individual superiority, loyalty, and fidelity, they overlooked the significance of the fact that one of them would prove before morning that he was the least worthy to claim such a high degree of faithfulness. And Jesus argued with them and rebuked them for the manner in which they were analyzing the situation.

He finally told them that this was the occasion when He was to fulfill His former great promises to them, and that at this very moment He appointed to each of them a kingdom just as His Father in Heaven had appointed a kingdom to Him, and that by this appointment they were to eat and drink at His table in His kingdom—or in other words to be co-equal with Him in this new Kingdom of Heaven on earth, in ruling it, directing it, and establishing it for all time in the future. They, as the twelve great Lights and leaders of the secret school guiding the scores of other faithful pupils who had been trained daily under Him, were to carry on His great mission in the future just as though He were present, speaking words of authority as He spoke them, and demonstrating powers that would be conferred upon them in the same manner that He had demonstrated in the past several years.

THE SECRET DOCTRINES OF JESUS

We all know from the various reports in the Gospels just what occurred after this great ceremony and secret meeting. He foretold how one of them would even deny Him several times before sunrise or before the cock would crow at the rising of the sun. He pictured to them the dire consequences of the following day and explained how this would be His day of agony, and that it would be followed by the greatest sacrifice He could make, that of giving up the Holy Ghost as the son of God and as the Christ on earth and being buried and entombed merely as a man while His great power and authority would continue to rest on them and with them. In some of the versions of this meeting, as presented to us by Matthew and Mark, there are slight modifications in the smaller details, but in general the story is the same with every bit of evidence that the Apostles and Jesus came together as representatives of a secret school or of a divine secret system of preparation, and that they met in a specially selected secret place and that He looked upon this occasion as the culminating act of transference of the sacred power and authority from Himself to the twelve Apostles. This transference of power and authority is perhaps more beautifully expressed by Matthew, Chapter 26, Verse 29, where it is recorded that

THE SECRET DOCTRINES OF JESUS

Jesus said, ". . . until that day when I drink it new with you in my Father's kingdom." The cup of wine was to be their last as well as His last under the conditions which existed, and they would never drink together again until the Kingdom of God had been established.

There was a previous occasion when such a secret meeting had been held for the purpose of closing the systematic course of instruction and series of demonstrations which He had given to His pupils in private and this had ended with a special ceremony of the transference of power and authority. We have perhaps the best story of this in the 9th chapter of Luke, without resorting to other older records outside of the Christian Bible. Here we learn that Jesus called His Disciples or students together and gave them power and authority over all the demons and the power to cure disease, and He sent them forth to proclaim the Kingdom of God and to heal the sick.

It is interesting to note here that the transference of power and authority constitute two separate transactions. In this case power does not mean authority or privilege. The power to heal and the power over unclean spirits refers to a definite, divine process applying divine principles and laws to material, physical, or spiritual conditions

THE SECRET DOCTRINES OF JESUS

in and around man. The students had to be prepared for the reception of this power that they might understand it and use it intelligently. It was not a mere formula or incantation or a chant, or some process of necromancy, or black magic or white magic such as the pagans had used.

The power which Jesus possessed was unique with Him and was the great gift of God the Father who sent Him. It consisted of knowledge that would prepare them, of days, weeks, and months of prayer and meditation that would purge them, and cleanse them, and make them proper receptacles and proper channels for the influx and outpouring of a divine principle which manifested itself as a unique and holy power to do certain things. And the authority which He granted to them, along with the power, also came from God, for without the authority the power would not have been released unto them and would not continue to flow through them.

As to the secret instructions which they were to follow in using this authority and power, we find that on this occasion when He called them together for the transference of His activities, He really qualified them to heal the sick and cleanse the lepers, to raise the dead, and to cast out devils. All Biblical authorities agree that this was truly

THE SECRET DOCTRINES OF JESUS

an occasion when the transmission of a supernatural power was made for the first time in the history of civilization. Now note that one of the principal points of the authority given them as quoted by Luke was to have power over all demons or devils, and according to other authorities, to have dominion over "unclean spirits."

Here we have reference to one of the secret doctrines, and it may be more logical to treat of this truth here and now than to place it among the other secret doctrines in the final chapters of this book.

It had been a common belief in ancient times among the uneducated and illiterate of the pagans and heathens that sickness of any kind, and especially that which seemed to break down the soundness of the inner parts of the body or the integrity and soundness of the mind and brain, was due to a form of obsession or to the presence in the body and in the brain of an evil spirit or demon that had deliberately or wilfully entered the physical body and was seeking to destroy it. At first only those who suffered from what we might term epilepsy or fits, or strange ravings and whirlings, and the throwing of themselves upon the ground were manifestations of "possession." For many centuries those who were unsound of mind and

THE SECRET DOCTRINES OF JESUS

who talked in a strange manner or whose memory failed them or who were imbeciles or verging upon loss of mental control, were suspected of being possessed by demons or controlled by devilish spirits. But eventually, every form of disease was attributed to some contact with unclean spirits.

The pagans had resorted to many very strange and superstitious practices in healing those who were in such conditions. A large majority were looked upon as hopeless and unworthy of being healed or cleansed, and were either buried alive or burned alive or tortured to death. It was even believed, at times in the past, that to come near one who was sick through being possessed, might cause a transference of the condition. For this reason it was difficult to find those who would even attempt to help them or to treat them. In some countries it was believed that if the shadow of a possessed one fell across your body you were contaminated.

It appears from ancient records also that certain types of men and women who seemed to understand that such beliefs were superstitious and who desired to commercialize their better understanding, classified themselves as magicians for the curing and healing of those who were suffering from possessions. They would offer—for large sums of material wealth—to take the unfortunate member of the family who was thus affected into their own homes and treat him and cure him, or at least look after him until he either became perfectly well or died. Analyzing the forms of treatment that were given to most of these unfortunate ones, it would seem that these professional magicians and healers, extremely wise as some of them were, were also tricksters and charlatans. Whenever one found it necessary to give an example of his methods of magical treatment in a public place, he would place the unfortunate or sick victim upon a couch of grass in the center of a large circle of public witnesses, including relatives of the victim, and proceed to chant with weird and mystical incantations, all the while walking around the sick one and sprinkling so-called holy water and other symbolical things upon the suffering body. Then he would take the patient to his home or hut and keep him in secret seclusion for a week or ten days, then bring him out into public and reveal him as perfectly cured.

The multitudes were always astonished by such procedures and the more often the demonstration was performed the more famous became the magician and the greater his income. It would appear, however, that these charlatans selected only those

THE SECRET DOCTRINES OF JESUS

who had diseases that nature would greatly assist in the course of time, or who might be helped through simple herbal remedies, for this was the only kind of patients that they would exhibit to the public. Those that they were called upon to cure who seemed to have some incurable disease, or some condition which nature did not quickly correct in the course of her usual activities, they refused to treat in public and would take to their secluded homes and keep for a long time and either eventually release as cured or return to their relatives or to a funeral pyre as dead.

It was through the practices of these charlatans, however, that the use of certain herbs, the sprinkling of water, and the chanting of incantations became a standard procedure much as we have standard procedures today in the cure of certain diseases.

These incantations, chanted very carefully and consistently with certain pagan rules and laws, utilized certain vowel sounds that were known to the ancients as being quieting to the nerves and inducive of sleep and relaxation. These formulas or chants of mystical vowel sounds, composed mostly of the vowels of very sacred and holy names which the public was not privileged to use without dire punishment, became the foundation for certain formulas and prayers and certain methods of chanting adopted later by the more evolved theological systems and introduced into the synagogues just before the Christian era and later introduced to the Christian church and carried on today in the form of sacred chants and hymns.

How far wrong were the Disciples of Jesus, and Jesus Himself, in believing that demons and devils and unclean spirits could take possession of the physical body and of the brain and bring about disease and unsound mental and physical conditions? The church of today ignores this question and Christianity today has wholly abandoned any consideration of the belief in evil spirits and demons taking possession of a healthy body and causing disease. Here is where we find great truths concealed under the cloak of ancient beliefs and thereby cast into oblivion.

The psychologists and psychiatrists today know that the human brain can become possessed or obsessed by certain beliefs and ideas which are gradually fixed in the human consciousness and dominate it. But it is generally conceded by them that such possessions and obsessions affect only the soundness of the mind and produce certain degrees or stages of insanity. Beyond that no modern physician or psychiatrist ventures to give an opinion.

THE SECRET DOCTRINES OF JESUS

But those who are deep and profound students of mysticism and of the mystical laws of the universe, and who have made themselves especially acquainted with the mysteries of the mind of man, know it is a fact that not only can the human mind become gradually possessed by fixed ideas, and therefore seemingly obsessed beyond external or internal control, but this obsession and possession can, and very often does, result in physical disturbances that later manifest as chronic diseases, the breaking down of tissue, the abnormal functioning of organs, and the eventual death of the body. It is a fact, therefore, that many forms of disease and abnormal conditions in the purely physical part of the body can be remedied or entirely eliminated by removing from the mind the evil "demon" or "devil" that possesses it or by removing the ideas of obsession that are fixed in the brain.

And it is possible to remove these mental obsessions and possessions, these fixed ideas and beliefs in the brain and mind of man, in the twinkling of the eye—or in a few hours—if the right procedure is followed. It has been demonstrated, and can easily be demonstrated by the properly trained and experienced practitioner, that an evil thought, which we might call a demon or a "possessing idea" that is like an hallucination or a devil in-

THE SECRET DOCTRINES OF JESUS

carnate in the mind, can be removed in a few days or even in a few hours with a resulting immediate change in the physical condition of the individual.

When the Christian Science doctrines attempt to explain the cause of physical illness as a mortal thought made manifest in the body because of its fixed possession of the mind, they are presenting in a modified dress and in a new form, one of the ancient beliefs, and they are correct in maintaining the claim that as a Christian religious institution they are the only representatives of the Christian doctrines attempting to carry out the work of the early Apostles. But it is not true that they are the only students of and practitioners of the ancient system of purging and cleansing the mind and the body of these evils and of casting out these devils and demons that are the cause of many forms of mental and physical illness. The Ancient Mystical Order Rosae Crucis (or the Rosicrucians) and other secret schools of real metaphysics and of mystical understanding in various parts of Europe and throughout the world, practice the ancient doctrines and teachings of Jesus and the Disciples without becoming religious movements or calling themselves members of a new church or a new form of religion.

THE SECRET DOCTRINES OF JESUS

The secret power of this doctrine lies in the fact that if the individual who is ill has faith in prayer to God (or to Jesus the Christ or His Apostles) to cleanse him of the demons and devils that are in possession of him, his attunement with God in sincere prayer, or his sympathetic cooperation with a physician, practitioner, or a mystic who is praying for him and with him, will bring about first a change in the mental condition which is the cause of the trouble, and immediately in the physical body where we see manifested the ultimate result of the demons in the mind and consciousness.

Prayer and faith in these circumstances constitute a purging process and this great secret, which Jesus taught to His Disciples and which they practiced, is one of the truly great secrets of Christian healing and of all pure metaphysical healing.

The Disciples learned from Jesus that prayers in the form of a chant, utilizing the vowel sounds which have a sympathetic effect upon the consciousness and the nervous system of the patient, are valuable assistants; and it is for this reason that in the mystical schools of today which are perpetuating the secret doctrines of Jesus—and in those churches which are attempting to perpetuate the ancient principles of the Disciples, chanting, and prayers in the form of a chant, and the use of vowel sounds remain as an important, a very important, curative process. Thus we see that Jesus secretly taught something to His Disciples which He did not make plain to the populace and which has not been carried down to the present time by the Christian religion as a fundamental part of the Christian teachings.

Again we say it is a fact that many forms of mental and physical unsoundness and disease are truly the result of mental obsessions and hallucinations, truthfully coming within the category of obsessions and possessions. In such cases it is useless to try to treat the body and the brain with medicines or any other form of therapy without purging the mind and resorting to the application of those secret laws which Jesus knew so well and which He used so professionally and expertly in His mission and throughout the years of His great work.

But we must pass on now to other proofs of the existence of the secret school and the work done in it by a larger number of Disciples and pupils than merely the twelve who constituted His private assembly or His secret board of councilors.

▽

Chapter VIII
THE GREATEST OF MIRACLES

▽

THERE was one miracle performed by Jesus that constitutes the greatest of all the miracles, regardless of the angle from which we view it. And the power to perform this miracle was transferred from Jesus to His Disciples with the understanding that the power to transfer it would pass to them also and that from master to student and from disciple to disciple throughout the ages this power to perform the greatest of miracles would be the divine inheritance of those who followed His teachings, developed His doctrines and evolved to the status of Christian fellowship. In the preachments of the Christian doctrines in modern times much is made of the assurance that the life of the redeemed and the life of the follower of Christian doctrines is immortal and that death will bring about merely a change in the place and condition of existence. There is nothing new in this doctrine of immortality for we find reference to it and many extreme forms of faith in it among the oldest of mystical and spiritual teachings and rituals. But

THE SECRET DOCTRINES OF JESUS

the manner in which Jesus revealed the law of immortality and then demonstrated it in His own life gave the doctrine a new form and a new interpretation.

It is not surprising, therefore, that the last great lesson which Jesus taught to His secret students, and demonstrated before His Apostles, was closely associated with His teaching of the doctrine of immortality. In fact, Jesus constantly gave emphasis to the fact that man could and would live again, and continually, if he but followed Him along the Path toward spiritual perfection. The Crucifixion of Jesus gave Him the glorious opportunity to prove His sincerity, His worthiness, and His absolute faith in the doctrines He taught. It permitted Him to demonstrate to His large number of students, and particularly to the Apostles, that He was willing to make the greatest of all sacrifices in behalf of the divine message and mission which it was His purpose to reveal to those who were ready to receive it.

While He was upon the Cross suffering the utmost of physical torment, and at the same time a victim of the mental torture and humiliation which accompanied it, He gave expression to words and terms that were intended to revive and

THE SECRET DOCTRINES OF JESUS

strengthen the faith His students had in His teachings and in the fulfillment of one of the great promises He had made to them.

He had promised them the miracle of all miracles, the guarantee of a power like unto His own, and a similar divine authority by which and through which they would be able to do the same things that He had done, and even greater things.

Around Him in that mortal throng of good and bad characters, wretched souls, doubting Thomases, scoffing witnesses, fearful officials, and awed believers, there were those who had reason to feel that this was the occasion of the closing of the last chapter of the life of Jesus and the cutting short of the glorious career each of them had anticipated. Truly, His sincere students and Disciples had lived and had their being in Him for months and years. Their faith in the future was a part of His faith. Their hope was based upon His hopes. Their ambitions, their desires, their determination to teach and demonstrate His doctrines in the future were contingent upon the success He made of His mission on earth. But here, now, the man who had cast out devils, removed the demons from the suffering bodies, made it possible for the halt to walk upright, and the blind to see, and even for the dead to rise from their death-

THE SECRET DOCTRINES OF JESUS

beds and live again, was about to be annihilated and removed forever from the face of the earth by His enemies, against whom He seemed unable to protect Himself or defend His faith and doctrines.

All was about to fall as His body became limp and lifeless. The spark of divine power which He held within His consciousness was about to be extinguished. In a few moments one of them—one of the most loyal and devoted of the secret students, known as Joseph—would carry out his promise of secretly protecting the abused and mutilated body by placing it in his elaborately arranged tomb, and the closing of the tomb would be the closing of the book of the life and teachings, the doctrines and miracles, of this greatest of all secret schools. No wonder the skies darkened and the clouds gathered together heavily, the lightning flashed, and the thunder rolled! Tomorrow would begin a dark cycle in the unfoldment of human existence on earth. It would be the beginning of the end and man would descend into hell as the Scriptures had prophesied.

But before the consciousness in the crucified body passed into sleep and the lips became silent, Jesus uttered again the assurance that He would enter the Kingdom of Heaven and continue to live

THE SECRET DOCTRINES OF JESUS

and that His promise to His secret students would be fulfilled. In silence and profound mystical understanding His scores of students and Apostles stepped out of the crowds and by devious routes reached the secret meeting place that they might come together in prayer and await that which they were sure would come on the morrow.

And on the morrow the word came that Jesus had disappeared from the tomb!

We can understand the surprise of the scoffers and the officials who realized that the responsibility for this unexpected occurrence might rest upon them. We can understand the awe in the minds and hearts of those who had been tempted to believe but needed just this additional demonstration to convince them. And we can also understand the silence and the increased faith that came into the hearts and souls of the students assembled in prayer not far from the site of the Crucifixion. They knew that if Jesus was no longer in the tomb, He was no longer unconscious, no longer "dead" in the sense that the officials had proclaimed and which the law considered sufficient. They knew that He still lived and that in due time, in accordance with an ancient ritual of resurrection which they had performed scores of times sym-

THE SECRET DOCTRINES OF JESUS

bolically in their secret temple, Jesus would appear again in their midst.

His continued invisibility to the multitudes strengthened their belief. According to the ancient Book of the Dead, and all the ancient rituals which they had reviewed in their secret studies, a certain number of days and nights must pass before the living Christ would be visible again. And so it occurred that after the definite number of days Jesus became visible to the objective, material consciousness of man and was first seen by one who loved Him, a woman. Her report fired again the faith and hope of the Disciples and they hurriedly assembled once more to await His coming. And so while they were together, the whole hundred or more of them, with the exception of Judas, with doors locked and windows and every portion of the premises under careful observation and protection, Jesus appeared in their midst. They questioned Him whether this was to be the occasion of the fulfillment of the great promise, the demonstration of the miracle of miracles, and He answered in terms that only the student of the ancient mysteries could understand then and now. He replied, "It is not for you to know the times or the seasons which the Father hath put in His own power!" In other words, He told them that it

THE SECRET DOCTRINES OF JESUS

was not for them to understand at the present time what time or what season, what hour or what moment, the great miracle would be performed, for they did not possess the power which His Father in Heaven possessed and which He had possessed up to the time of His Crucifixion, but which He had surrendered while on the cross. That power had returned to its divine source and was possessed by no man at that moment.

But Jesus spoke again to assure them that this did not mean the abandonment of His plans nor the crushing of their hope. His words were symbolical but definite: "But ye shall receive power when the Holy Spirit cometh upon you: and ye shall be witnesses to me, in Jerusalem, and in all Judea and Samaria, and to the extremity of the earth." (Acts, Chapter I.) These words are similarly expressed in several records and contain the mystical keys to a great divine formula. He had greeted them with the mystical salutation of "Peace be unto you!" typifying and illustrating what He meant at a previous mystical ceremony. He showed them the injured and mutilated parts of His body to prove that the body was in fact "broken" as He had broken the bread and given it to them, and He showed them the blood flowing

THE SECRET DOCTRINES OF JESUS

from His wounds as was symbolized by the wine that He had poured from the cup.

Then He performed the first part of the miracle of miracles. It was not the culminating act which they were looking for, but the first step in a ceremonial procedure that had its ritualism written in the consciousness of God and decreed by Him. While they knelt in the form of two interlaced triangles within a circle in the same manner in which they had knelt on many occasions, He raised His hands while standing in the center of the mystical form and said again, "Peace be unto you: as my Father hath sent me, even so send I you." These are the words which St. John gives in the 20th chapter of his Book, but in other records we read that Jesus said, "Peace be unto you! In the same manner in which my Father sent me and transferred unto me the power of the Holy Spirit, I now ordain you and prepare you to receive the power of the Holy Ghost that was mine."

According to the Books of the New Testament, Jesus then "breathed on them and said to them, Receive the Holy Spirit. Whose soever sins ye remit, they are remitted to them; whose soever ye redeem, they are redeemed."

The breathing on them was a very sacred and divine procedure. It was the only occasion during

THE SECRET DOCTRINES OF JESUS

the whole history of the life of Jesus and during His whole ministry that He had ever breathed upon another human being, and it was the only occasion upon which He had ever officially said in connection with such a ceremony or any mystical ceremony, "Receive ye the Holy Spirit!" Here was the first act of the miracle of miracles. It is to be noted that Jesus did not say, "I give unto you the power of the Spirit!" or, "I transfer to you from me the power of the Holy Spirit and it now abideth in thee." The Holy Ghost and the power of it were no longer possessed by Jesus for He had given it up while on the Cross. But as the divine messenger of the Father He was the channel through which the Holy Ghost did move from the Father to the Disciples. Breathing upon them was merely the preparation for the incoming or the downcoming of the Holy Ghost, and Jesus simply told them that they were to be immediately aware of receiving it.

The rest of the formula used by Jesus regarding the remission of sins was a part of the secret doctrines which they clearly understood. The key to the explanation of this formula will be found only in the doctrine of Karma as secretly taught by Jesus to His Disciples and Apostles and touched

THE SECRET DOCTRINES OF JESUS

upon allegorically in some of the parables and injunctions given by Jesus to the multitudes.

It is to be noted that in all the strictly orthodox interpretations of this mystical formula as discussed and analyzed and commented upon in the most authentic and recognized of commentaries and Biblical encyclopedias, the attitude is taken that this formula did not confer upon the Disciples or the Apostles the right to forgive or remit sin. It is claimed by the writers of such reverent books that the power to remit sins was never exercised by one of the Apostles and plainly was never understood by themselves as possessed by them or conveyed to them. Some ecclesiastical authorities go so far as to say that "the power to intrude upon the relation between man and God cannot have been given by Christ to His ministers in any but a ministerial or declarative sense."

But this is an error of opinion due to the fact that the mystical nature of the formula was concealed by the Disciples themselves, and is but one of the many secret doctrines of Jesus which the Christian church of today has forgotten or misunderstood. The misinterpretation or misunderstanding of this formula is partly responsible for the opinion on the part of many thousands of Christians that the priest of the Roman Catholic

THE SECRET DOCTRINES OF JESUS

Church has the power in the name of Jesus the Christ to forgive or remit sins. Yet if this power had never been transferred to the Disciples it could not have been transferred to the fathers of the Roman Catholic Church and by them to the priesthood.

According to the Law of Karma, as one of the secret doctrines, Jesus said to His Disciples—in connection with the incoming of this power of the Holy Ghost which would enable them to perform miracles and to carry on His great mission—that whose soever sins they remitted would be remitted to them as a Karmic debt for which they must make compensation; that while the sins would be forgiven they would not be forgotten and could not be completely remitted until the individuals themselves had made compensation for each sin; and, on the other hand, whose soever sins they redeemed or refrained from forgiving, the Disciples themselves would have to carry as a Karmic debt for which they would have to make compensation and adjustment. In other words, if the Disciples forgave the sins of an individual, that individual had to carry the responsibility for compensation as his cross, and until he lightened the burden of the cross by complete compensation the remitted sins rested upon him. But if the Disciple in his judg-

THE SECRET DOCTRINES OF JESUS

ment refused to remit the sins of an individual and decided that they were too great, too heavy, or that the individual was unworthy or undeserving of such remission or forgiveness, the Disciple by thus acting as judge and sitting in judgment upon another, assumed the responsibility of the Karmic debt along with the sinner.

In the secret doctrines taught by Jesus, and later transmitted to the mystery schools of today, this same formula is expressed in this manner: If the one having the power and the Holy Ghost to aid and assist the sinner can point out to him the manner in which he can purge himself of his sins by making compensation and thus removing the stain upon his soul and consciousness, he transfers the burden of the sin from the divine consciousness or divine records to the consciousness of the sinner with the understanding that if the sinner purges himself of his sins by making proper compensation, he relieves himself of the Karmic cross or burden and thus becomes cleansed and prepared for redemption. But he who dares to withhold such knowledge and such advice as will enable the sinner to purge himself by making compensation and cleansing his soul of his sins, thereby sitting in final judgment upon him and *deeming* him unworthy of redemption, becomes the holder of the

THE SECRET DOCTRINES OF JESUS

unremitted sins and the Karmic debt is his, and he in time must make compensation for these sins or suffer the consequences along with the sinner.

With this formula is coupled the ancient and mystical injunction that he who is on the Path or walking in the Light and in a position to give spiritual aid and guidance to another, and who dares to sit in judgment upon another and decide that one sinner or another is too sinful for redemption or beyond the pale of the remittance of his sins, then becomes not only a sinner, but, daring to sit in judgment upon his brother, assumes a responsibility and must carry with the sinner the burden of the Karma that he has thus taken upon himself by his judgment. He is enjoined, therefore, not to attempt to judge (or *deem*) his brothers, not to attempt to say that any sinner is unworthy of the remission of his sins, for instantly he becomes a partner in the sins and must share with the sinner the burden of his cross.

After this definite instruction, they moved silently with Jesus out into the stillness of the setting sun and assembled again in a cave beneath a great rock where the last rites of their mystical ceremony for this occasion were followed by prayer, chanting, and ceremonial action.

THE SECRET DOCTRINES OF JESUS

Then the large assembly dispersed and Jesus and His eleven Apostles, remaining alone, moved up to the top of the rock beneath which they had been assembled, formed themselves into a circle and Jesus stood in the center. While they folded their arms in a mystical salutation with the right hand over the left breast, and with their feet in the correct position, symbolical of their ritualism, a cloud formed in the center of the circle. This did not surprise them, for the forming of such a cloud had been witnessed by them on many occasions and they knew the law whereby it was formed and anticipated that after the power to do this and other things had been conferred upon them, they too would form such clouds on occasions. The ancient schools of mysticism and divine science have practiced the formation of this formula and process for many ages and its secret is still in practice in the mystical schools of today. When such clouds are formed those who are in the midst of them become invisible, but in this case Jesus became not only invisible but as the cloud arose He appeared to arise with it. At a certain height above them the cloud gradually dissolved and the spiritual form of Jesus as well as the physical form disappeared.

THE SECRET DOCTRINES OF JESUS

As the Apostles watched this strange demonstration of divine power there came upon them as an influx of the divine power the Holy Ghost. It descended upon them as it had descended upon Jesus on the occasion of His Baptism. This was the miracle of miracles, for with its descent the eleven Apostles became the living inheritors of the divine power which Jesus had possessed, transferable by them in the same manner to the worthy, and used by them in the spread of their mission and the mission of Jesus for the redemption of man.

▽

Chapter IX
MORE BIBLICAL VERIFICATION

▽

NDOUBTEDLY many of my readers, and possibly a large number of very devout Christians, will question the authenticity of my statements regarding the number of actual Disciples or students and intimate followers who were a part of the secret school organized and directed by Jesus.

The common belief is that Jesus had twelve intimates who were not only the twelve Apostles but also the only personal, private students ever instructed by Him, and therefore the only ones who could have been in possession of any secret teachings that He might have revealed. Therefore, my statement that there were a hundred and twenty in His private school, including the twelve Apostles, will demand Biblical verification.

I trust I may be pardoned at this point for diverging for a moment from the general theme to take up a tangent one; namely, the demand for authenticity and verification exclusively from the Bible.

THE SECRET DOCTRINES OF JESUS

Many eminent clergymen—and hundreds of devout Bible students—who have read my previous book, *The Mystical Life of Jesus,* have written me long letters demanding that I furnish proof, or at least some form of substantiation, of many of the statements made in that book. But in each and every case they have demanded that the verification or authentication or partial supporting evidence be taken from the Christian Bible or from "the Holy Scriptures" as they prefer to classify that source of information.

It has seemed strange to me that anyone who is demanding truth should at the same time qualify its source and limit and classify the channel of its expression. After all, is there no other source of historical evidence, no other form of authentical knowledge pertaining to the Christian times and the Christian doctrines than that which is in the Christian Bible or Holy Scriptures? If that is true, why are Christian theologians and Christian fathers, and the world's most eminent theological researchers combing every part of ancient history and every section of ancient lands for what they call cumulative evidence, historical evidence, or mute evidence to verify the statements made in the Bible? If evidence can be found outside of the Christian Bible, why then

THE SECRET DOCTRINES OF JESUS

limit all authentication or support of Christian historical statements solely and exclusively to the Christian Bible? And if nothing except that which is in black and white in the words of the Christian Bible is reliable or dependable, or acceptable in connection with anything pertaining to the life of Christ or His teachings and activities, then why all of this research and why this age-old hunt, these costly explorations, and this laborious study and analysis of ancient writings in the hope of finding more and more facts that throw light upon Christian history and Christian doctrines?

If everything pertaining to the life of Christ and the Christian institutions must be taken from the Christian Bible in order to be authentic and dependable, *then nothing more than the Christian Bible need ever be written* regarding the life of Christ and His teachings. Yet, thousands of books have been written interpreting, analyzing, and explaining the passages in the Christian Bible, and thousands of books have been written in all languages quoting from historical evidence, from mute evidence, from all forms of evidence found outside of the Christian Bible supporting or tending to support and cast new light upon the statements in the Christian Bible.

THE SECRET DOCTRINES OF JESUS

Much has been written by Biblical authorities regarding the historical writings of Josephus, and the magnifying glass has been applied to every passage in his works, accompanied by arguments as to whether they do or do not confirm or verify statements in the Christian Bible about Jesus and His great work. Why look to the book by Josephus and why even quote anything he says, if, after all, the only reliable and dependable verification may be found in the New Testament?

But, of course, it is a mistaken idea on the part of those who have established a prejudicial and biased attitude toward the subject to claim that the only dependable evidence is that which is to be found in the Christian Bible. Much that is in the Christian Bible would not be understandable today if it were not for light thrown upon many of its passages by external evidence. Historical research, and in fact research in every branch of the sciences and arts has tended to cast new light upon parts of the Bible and has given verification or modification to some of the puzzling passages. Almost monthly, and certainly yearly, during the past few centuries, explorations—geological, geographical, astronomical, and historical—have given us much new knowledge or verified much old knowledge regarding Jesus and His time, His teachings and

THE SECRET DOCTRINES OF JESUS

His marvelous mission. But those who are biased, and yet believe themselves to be sincere and honest students of Biblical research and Christian truths, refuse to accept any external evidence that does not minutely support and verify every word and every passage in the old versions and the modern versions of the Christian Bible.

Still, Biblical research itself, carried on for centuries by groups and officially selected bodies of translators and interpreters, has constantly brought us new interpretations, new versions, new understandings of many of the passages of the Bible. The King James version, now so commonly accepted, was quite a modification in some important points, of the former accepted interpretations and versions of the Books of the Bible. And in very recent times many of the significant and important words or passages in the Synoptic Gospels have been greatly changed and modified, sometimes to an extreme degree. If such modifications and changes are permissible and acceptable, then we must admit that every period, every comma, and every word in many of the old or recent versions may be questioned some day and should not be accepted today as the unquestionable truth which must either be completely verified by any external evidence or such evidence completely rejected.

THE SECRET DOCTRINES OF JESUS

To demand that a book such as this, or such as *The Mystical Life of Jesus,* should have every statement conform to the statements in the Christian Bible means that the author should have merely rewritten the Christian Bible in precisely its same words *or written nothing at all!* Such an attitude would exclude the possibility of any new light ever being cast upon the manifold mysteries which surround the life and the teachings of Jesus the Christ.

To return to our main theme, however, it is fortunate that in this particular case we find evidence in the generally accepted and adopted versions of the Christian Bible to support and verify my statements regarding the actual number of students and intimate co-workers in the secret school conducted by Jesus.

If we turn to the Book of the Acts of the Apostles and read, beginning with the 12th verse of the first chapter, what the Disciples and followers proceeded to do after the Crucifixion, Burial, and Ascension of Jesus, we find that on a certain day they left the Mount of Olives and secretly went up again to their private meeting room or schoolroom and assembled in the usual manner. The 13th verse of this chapter plainly indicates that they returned to the meeting place in which

THE SECRET DOCTRINES OF JESUS

they were accustomed to assemble at that period of time. In other words, they did not assemble in a new place or an unaccustomed place but a place where they had been remaining for a time. Whether it was the identical meeting place in which the Last Supper had been held, or where previous ceremonies had been held in secrecy is not indicated, but they did not meet on this occasion in a new place. The 13th and 14th verses tell us who the principal ones were who assembled there. It says that there were: "Peter, and James, and John, and Andrew, Philip, and Thomas, Bartholomew, and Matthew, James the son of Alpheus, and Simon Zelotes, and Judas the brother of James. All these continued with one accord in prayer and supplication, with the women, and Mary the mother of Jesus, and with His brethren."

We see in these two verses that not only were the Apostles present but "the women" and also Mary, the mother of Jesus, and His brethren—the actual blood and flesh brothers of Jesus.

Perhaps many Christian students will be surprised at the foregoing words, for in the 14th verse—quoted above—there are three real surprises for a great many. The first is that among the Apostles and Disciples and students of Jesus who met secretly there were women. There are a

THE SECRET DOCTRINES OF JESUS

number of passages in the Bible which intimate that women were not excluded from the secret discipleship of the original school established by Jesus.

Not long ago in discussing the life and activities of Jesus with a very eminent and elderly patriarch and priest of the Greek Catholic Church I asked him what, in his opinion, was one of the outstanding and unique features of the Christian church as compared with the ancient religions and the contemporary religions at the time of Jesus. After some minutes of deep thought, he said he believed it was the position that the Christian church gave to women, and the recognition of equal rights which the Christian church gave to women through the attitude that Jesus held toward them. The more one analyzes this thought, the more apparently true it becomes. Up to the time that Jesus accepted women on an equal basis with men under His cloak and took them into His consideration as human beings possessing souls, women held a very lowly, humble, and even unrecognized position in most religions and in the religious movements of Palestine.

It has often been said that Jesus was either never in love or else so deeply in love that He did not allow Himself to refer to it as a human emotion.

THE SECRET DOCTRINES OF JESUS

It has been claimed by blinded readers of Christian doctrines, or by those who read the Christian Bible through colored glasses, that Jesus never gave a single human thought to womankind. Others have claimed that Jesus looked upon them with total indifference. Still others have tried to make much of the fact that a woman bathed His feet on one occasion, and at the Crucifixion women indicated their love and adoration for Him. There are passages in the Christian Bible which would indicate that on occasions Jesus felt very friendly toward certain women, and talked with them in a manner to indicate that He held them in much higher esteem than they were held by the majority of men in His day. And it must be remembered that He permitted Himself to be seen by a woman for the first time after His Crucifixion and Resurrection. Call that meeting "accidental" if you choose, but such a thought belittles all the powers of Jesus, for in the light of His other miracles and His hundreds of other acts we must be convinced that He could have avoided such an "accidental" meeting with a woman if He had preferred to have His first visible manifestation of Resurrection made to one of His Apostles.

Not only does His attitude toward the Scarlet Woman indicate that He had a sympathetic un-

THE SECRET DOCTRINES OF JESUS

derstanding of the problems of womankind, especially in those days and under such civil and moral codes, and that He had a tenderness and a kindness at heart for all women and especially the unfortunate, but many other passages indicate that women held a very distinct place of recognition in His life, though He realized very keenly their limitations under the existing codes. With all of the understanding and power, authority and instructions He might give them they still would have been unable to carry out His mission with the same freedom of movement and expression granted to His Apostles.

So, to many, the surprise in this verse may be the statement that there were women among His many secret students. From all of the ancient records dealing with the organization and maintenance of secret schools we cannot doubt that there were an equal number of men and women among the students of this Christian school, and that, except for the degree of Apostleship limited to the Twelve by the codes and customs and regulations of the country, Jesus would have given to such women as were qualified, equal power and authority with the men.

The next surprising fact is that among these women in the secret school was Mary, His mother.

THE SECRET DOCTRINES OF JESUS

This is the last mention in the Christian Bible of Mary, the mother of Jesus. That she was an apt student, qualified even from birth to become as great an Apostle or Disciple as any that He selected, is shown in my book, *The Mystical Life of Jesus*. We are often told by those who pretend to be, or claim to be, profound students of Bible history that not only was Jesus totally indifferent toward women and preferred to have none of them around Him, but in support of this argument it is pointed out that He even rebuked His mother on one occasion and told her not to bother Him about coming home but to go on her way and leave Him alone because He had important business to attend to in connection with His Father's divine instructions. That seeming rebuke, given when He was a young man, is magnified and enlarged upon with a wholly erroneous interpretation.

If it were not for the particular verse in the first chapter of the Acts of the Apostles, it might be worth while to quote many other passages showing that Jesus was not unkindly and impatiently rebuking His mother when He spoke in such a manner on the occasion of His visit to the synagogue. But the fact that Mary was one of His secret, private, trusted students and Disciples on an equal basis with all the others plainly indicates that He was never impatient with her and did not look upon her as being unworthy of His companionship or lacking in understanding of His mission in life.

And the third surprise in that 14th verse is in the last four words—"and with His brethren." In many places throughout the Christian Bible reference is made to the brethren of Jesus and it has been common practice for many preachers and theologians and Scriptural analysts to attempt to explain that *all of mankind* represented the "brethren" of Jesus, and that He was accustomed to refer to all who stood about Him and who were of the male sex as His brethren, and that He particularly referred to His Disciples and Apostles as His brethren—never with the intention of meaning His brothers in flesh and blood. But in this case Jesus is not using the word, *brethren;* one of His followers is using it in a manner in which it is used in several other places in the Bible and which cannot be interpreted in any other but the correct manner. If we turn, for instance, to the 13th chapter of Matthew, and the 55th verse, we read: "Is not this the carpenter's son? Is not His mother called Mary? and His brethren, James and Joseph and Simon and Judas?"

THE SECRET DOCTRINES OF JESUS

To those who may be surprised that Jesus had a number of brothers there will be another surprise when we refer to His sisters. Yet in the very next verse in this 13th chapter of Matthew, we read: "And His sisters, are they not all with us?"

Turning to Chapter 7 of the Book of John, the 10th verse, we read: "But when His brethren were gone up, then He also Himself went up to the feast, not openly, but as it were in secret." Here again we have an unquestionable reference to His brothers of the flesh. In proof of this let us recall the story that this 7th chapter of John is telling.

As in many families where there is a prophet or a genius, a wizard or a Light among Men, the other members of the household may look with doubt and skepticism upon the claims, or the pretensions, or even the manifest acts and wisdom of the other; so in the case of Jesus. Early in His career the members of His family, except His mother, probably questioned the greatness and even the divinity of His mission. They may even have ridiculed or scoffed at His early preachings. This chapter of John is telling us how Jesus moved about in the open even after He had been warned that the Jews and others sought to kill Him. So in the third verse of this chapter we are told that His brethren therefore said to Him, "Depart hence

THE SECRET DOCTRINES OF JESUS

and go into Judea that Thy Disciples also may behold Thy works which Thou doest."

Then in the next verse we are told that "His Brethren" said: "For no man doeth anything in secret and Himself seeketh to be known openly. If Thou doest these things, manifest Thyself to the world." And in the next verse, the 5th, we read: "For even His brethren did not believe on Him."

We see in these verses that a distinction is clearly made in Verse 3 between His brethren and His Disciples and the reference to His brethren not believing on Him could not refer to the Disciples. And in Verse 8, Jesus told His brethren to go on up to the feast and that He would appear later.

Taking all of the foregoing into consideration we see that Verses 13 and 14 of the first chapter of the Acts of the Apostles give us considerable evidence regarding what was going on in the very private periods of the life of Jesus when He was making His plans and carrying out His mission in secrecy with His school of students.

If my reader is surprised to find that His mother and many women and His brothers, and no doubt His sisters, were among His private students, the next great surprise will probably be in the following verse, the 15th, where we read: "And in those

THE SECRET DOCTRINES OF JESUS

days Peter arising in the midst of the Disciples, said, (the number of the names together was about an hundred and twenty)." Before stating what Peter said to them let us note the definiteness with which this verse presents the facts that the number of those assembled in this secret meeting, including the mother and His brothers and women generally, was about an hundred and twenty. Certainly this does not limit the number to the Twelve, and we see in this 15th verse that Peter arose in the midst of the "Disciples" who included the "brethren" of Jesus as explained in the 14th verse. The distinction between these two terms is again very significant.

Now, the occasion for this meeting of all of the members of the secret school was an important matter. We notice that the 14th verse said that all of those thus assembled "continued with one accord in prayer and supplication." We find in the first verse of the 2nd chapter of the Book of the Acts reference again to the fact that "they were all with one accord in one place," and in the 46th verse of the same chapter we read that they continued daily "with one accord in the temple." In other places we find reference to this meeting "in the temple" as in the 53rd verse of the 24th chapter of Luke.

THE SECRET DOCTRINES OF JESUS

This meeting place in an *upper room,* as it is referred to in the Book of the Acts, this secret meeting place to which they were accustomed to go, was their "secret temple," a term used in antiquity by the secret schools of all ages. In fact, the word *temple* to indicate a limited, secluded, sacred meeting place was first used by the early mystery schools, and the word used by them is most correctly interpreted into the modern word derived from the Latin—*temple.* That is why in most of the secret societies and fellowships of the world today, and especially among those devoted to a study of the sacred philosophies and sacred mysteries, the holy of holies is still called the *temple.*

The occasion for this special meeting was the election of another Apostle to take the place of Judas who had betrayed Jesus and who had suffered the loss of his earthly life as a result of his attempt to escape from his own conscience. So we find that Peter arose in the midst of this meeting and addressed them after long prayers and supplications with the following thoughts: "It was necessary that the Holy Scripture of the past and the prophecies of our ancient days should be fulfilled as the Holy Spirit had revealed to us by the mouth of David concerning a Judas who was to guide the enemies to the correct place where they might find

THE SECRET DOCTRINES OF JESUS

our great leader and Saviour Jesus. This terrible manifestation of treason and treachery, or disloyalty and enmity, had to be fulfilled. It was decreed that Jesus should come to His timely end through the treachery of a Judas. He had been one with us, our companion, our trusted associate, but His part had been allotted to Him in the service that we were to render individually and collectively. And so it came about that one of our companions performed the necessary but regrettable act and then with the wages of his iniquity, with the bag of gold that he received, he purchased a field. And in running through it to escape from those who might see him and recognize him, and to escape the mockery of his conscience, he ran across the field to hide and in doing so he fell and injured himself and brought death to himself, and he bled profusely upon the field even to such an extent that all who heard of it at once nicknamed the field Aceldama, which means *a field of blood*."

"You will recall," said Peter to the assembly, "that it is written in the Book of Psalms, 'Let his habitation become desolate and let no man dwell in it: and let another take his office.'"

Then Peter explained to them that the vacancy in their midst must be filled by one who could be a witness to all of the acts of Jesus—even a witness

THE SECRET DOCTRINES OF JESUS

of His Crucifixion and His Resurrection. Therefore they must choose as a successor to Judas one who had been a companion with them all the time that Jesus had been in and around and among them. So they selected two who could fill the position, the one being Joseph called Barsabas, and who was surnamed Justus, and another called Matthias. After more prayer in which they petitioned God who knew the hearts of all of them to show them which of the two had been selected on high to take up the part of the ministry and Apostleship which Judas had deserted, they finally voted with ballots and the selection fell to Matthias, and he was numbered with the other eleven Apostles to make the number of twelve complete.

If we only knew all the names of those who were members of the secret school, many of the mysteries connected with the life of Jesus might be solved. We have found, for instance, that Joseph of Arimathea was a Disciple of Jesus but a very secret one, according to the Book of John, Chapter 19, Verse 38. According to other sources of information, this Joseph was a rich and pious Israelite who had the privilege of performing the last offices of duty and affection to the body of Jesus. He is clearly distinguished from any other Joseph by the addition of his birthplace to

THE SECRET DOCTRINES OF JESUS

his name. In Mark, the 15th chapter, 43rd verse, we learn that Joseph was a very honorable councilor, by which we are to understand that he was a member of the great Council of Sanhedrin. This makes evident the reason for the secrecy of his connection with the private school of Jesus and why he was referred to as a secret Disciple. In Luke, Chapter 23, Verse 50, we learn that he was a good and just man and one of those who, bearing in their hearts the words of their old prophets, were waiting for the Kingdom of God. We are told very clearly in the Bible that Joseph did not consent to the counsel and deed of his colleagues in conspiring to bring about the death of Jesus. But it does seem as though he lacked some courage that would have forced him to openly protest against their judgment. On the other hand, knowing the secret agreement and pledge taken by all of the Disciples of the great school, we know that there were occasions when silence was enforced upon them, and when they were forbidden to protest, and especially to exercise any political power or influence to divert the Cosmic course of events.

If the Crucifixion, Resurrection, and Ascension of Jesus were preordained and even His betrayal preordained, there would have been little use in

THE SECRET DOCTRINES OF JESUS

having Joseph reveal his relationship to Jesus and the secret school by futilely protesting against an event that was preordained. But we understand now why Joseph went boldly into the presence of Pilate and requested that the body of Jesus be turned over to him, and some day we may learn just why Pilate was so reluctant to carry on the great farce of a trial and the resulting crime, and also why he was so ready to consent to the request of Joseph.

Another important point in connection with the services rendered by Joseph will be of interest to all Rosicrucians and to all mystics of the ancient mystery schools. We are told that this rich man possessed a great tomb hewn in a great rock and that it was a tomb "where no human corpse had ever yet been laid" and that it was located in a garden that also belonged to Joseph and "close to the place of Crucifixion." However, the symbolism here will not be missed. The tomb—in which no one had ever been laid—in a great rock, in a garden, was more than just an ordinary tomb. In many centuries the mystery schools have used such tombs into which the bodies of their great leaders are placed only to be resurrected. The tomb in which Jesus was placed by Joseph was partially reserved for the secret school. It may

THE SECRET DOCTRINES OF JESUS

have been in a garden owned by Joseph and it may be that being a rich and pious member of the secret school he donated the tomb to the school, but a part of it never was intended for an ordinary person or for an ordinary burial, and it was known at the time that Joseph and his friend Nicodemus "infolded the body of Jesus in the linen shroud [knowing] that Jesus would rise from the tomb."

In passing it may be interesting to note that this same Joseph was sent to Great Britain by the Apostle St. Philip about the year 63 and settled there at Glastonbury with a few other Disciples from the secret school. Here he continued with them their special missions assigned to them by Jesus and representing the Christian institutions and laying the foundation for the teachings and practices of the secret doctrines.

I trust that I have given in this chapter sufficient Biblical evidence of the existence of a unique fellowship or society, to satisfy even the most analytical student of the Bible. But I have no hope of having satisfied the average Christian clergyman or priest.

I find from very careful research that many theologians in the past have ventured to express the opinion, and often the positive statement, that the actual number of true followers or Disciples of Jesus was 70. This number was derived from certain statements in the Bible wrongly interpreted or accepted without consideration of other facts. Moreover, it is contradictory to the statement quoted above regarding the presence of one hundred and twenty Disciples on the occasion of the election of a successor to Judas. Some theologians have admitted that they have found evidence in reading and rereading the early Jewish records and Greek records that Joseph of Arimathea was one of the seventy secret Disciples.

But it is very evident that in addition to the twelve Apostles of whom so much is said in all modern Christian preachments, there was a large number of Disciples who did not hold the official position of Apostles. The fact, then, that the following of Jesus was divided into a large body of Disciples with an inner body or circle of twelve Apostles, immediately presents to us a definite picture of the ancient system of a secret society and secret fellowship. Any argument that may be forthcoming from critics of this book to the effect that the only reason there were secret Disciples was because Jesus was in hiding or attempting to hide from His enemies, and His Disciples also had to remain secret in order to protect their lives, is

THE SECRET DOCTRINES OF JESUS

outbalanced by the fact that it was only in the latter period of Jesus' activities that He attempted any secrecy regarding His whereabouts or that He found it necessary for Himself or His Disciples to move and act in secret. Yet these one hundred and twenty Disciples were so well trained and so well qualified that they were authorized and empowered to continue His activities, to carry out His mission, and to do the miraculous things that He had done.

Are we to believe, therefore, that these one hundred and twenty secret Disciples became Disciples secretly only in the last year of the life of Jesus? Are we to believe that they could have become well trained and well qualified in even less than a year? The only possible explanation for the power and authority given to them and the intimate relationship which they had with Jesus up to the very last day is that they had been well trained for a long period of time, and if this is so why is it that no mention is made of the activities of these hundred and twenty Disciples in the early years of the life of Jesus while they were His students and co-workers? The only conclusion is that they were secret members from the very beginning and were not intended to be referred to in connection with the work of Jesus until such condi-

THE SECRET DOCTRINES OF JESUS

tions arose in the last year that necessitated a revelation of their existence and of their activities and participation in the last events of His life. This being true, His group of Disciples would constitute a typical secret society and a typical secret school; and the ritualism of their ceremonies, their methods of entering the secret meeting place, the strange signs which they used for identification and for greeting, all resemble, and, in fact, duplicate the mystical processes, ceremonies, signs, and greetings of several of the very ancient mystery schools that were unquestionably secret societies teaching and promulgating the ancient wisdom and secret doctrines.

This conclusion is further strengthened by the doctrines themselves—the doctrines which Jesus taught openly, and in which the parables and allegories contain recognizable symbols, and the doctrines which He taught His Disciples and which they carried on and preserved as the foundation of the present Christian church. Therefore, our next duty is to examine these ancient doctrines and see in them the very definite relationship to the ancient secret teachings, the unquestionable foundation of them in the mysteries of other schools, and the secret of the power which Christianity possessed in those doctrines which have not been inculcated and put into practice in the modern forms of the Christian religion.

▽

Chapter X

THE SECRET DOCTRINES

▽

T WOULD require a very large volume, in size and form of an encyclopedia, to outline each and every one of the secret doctrines and principles expounded and demonstrated by Jesus in His secret school during the course of its existence. There is some evidence that a large number of minor principles were abandoned during the first few months of the school's existence while a large number of other minor principles were united into triunes or groups of three principles to form a fundamental doctrine, and a number of the ultimate doctrines were eventually modified and laid aside because they were not appropriate, propitious, and applicable to the unique conditions and times, and would have little or no value in other countries in future years.

The best that can be done to cover this subject adequately, and give the reader and student a basic and comprehensive understanding of the essential secrets, is to select those which have come down to us through the ages in either their pristine or original form or slightly modified, or which have been withdrawn from public exposition since the second or third century and kept wholly within a certain inner circle of the Christian priesthood or Hierarchy.

Perhaps the most fundamental, the most interesting, and the most revolutionary of all of the radical principles taught by Jesus, and which became the basis for a number of His doctrines, was that pertaining to His moral code. It is generally acknowledged that the moral element of the Christian code is more or less ideal, but unquestionably an outstanding feature, a workable one with hidden subtle qualities and effects, and not comprehended by the average Christian and certainly incompletely and inadequately revealed by Christian preachers and teachers.

Very early in the missionary work of Jesus and throughout His entire career He gave great emphasis to the matter of morality. But His code of morals appeared to be astonishingly strange to the old philosophers and religionists. Perhaps only the mystics of the day saw in His moral code a very familiar principle. But it was by this moral code that Jesus measured the standard and quality of the character and nature of those individuals whom He admitted into the secret school. It was His yardstick by which He determined the fitness of

THE SECRET DOCTRINES OF JESUS

those individuals who became interested in His teachings and expressed sufficient interest to warrant being invited to join with others in more personal and intimate contact with His society.

The thought has often been expressed by those who have analyzed the Christian doctrines, in comparison with ancient pagan religions, that the religion and teachings of Jesus constituted a morality that was higher than that established or acknowledged by the pagans or tribal peoples throughout the world. But this is a mistaken idea due to a misunderstanding of the real nature of the ancient moral code and the real mystery element in the moral code that Jesus established. We shall see that Jesus did not create this moral code, that it was not unique with Him, having existed in the mystery schools for many ages, but it was something that was considered understandable and applicable only by those of spiritual development and mystical unfoldment. To preach it in some subtle form and gradually to establish it as a common code among the common people was indeed a profound and seemingly impossible task that Jesus set for Himself—or which was preordained for Him.

Among the ancient people and among the pagans, even in His own day, the moral code generally accepted and in application was a form of rules

THE SECRET DOCTRINES OF JESUS

or regulations directing the individuals to pay respect to the requirements and necessities and the more or less universal needs of the community. Such a moral code constituted a sort of civic duty toward one's neighbor or toward one's community. It was wholly an impersonal thing. It was based upon the fact that the essential element of man's existence insofar as personal conduct was concerned was the outer objective self of man. It was the natural or unnatural, normal or abnormal, pleasures of the flesh that tempted man into most of the sins he committed and led to the greatest degree, the greatest expressions, of immorality. In nearly all of the ancient scriptural writings can be found allegories of some kind, often almost identical with the story of the fall of man as expressed in the Old Testament. This temptation to partake of the fruits of the earth through the intriguing whisperings and urges of the serpent (which creature in symbolism always represented the subtle voice of earthly things and the subtle nature of worldly expression) typified the thought and idea that all sin and certainly all immorality was of the outer man through his mortal, worldly senses. Even the "sin of all sins," and the greatest sin of all, and any so-called "sin against a god" were of the outer self.

THE SECRET DOCTRINES OF JESUS

It must be understood, however, that in the comprehension and understanding of the pagan and the primitive peoples and of most of the intelligent and philosophically inclined of the period, there was no such term of distinction as the *outer* self. There was but one manifest, tangible, visible *self*. This was the body and brain and mortal senses of man. The existence of a soul within that body was, indeed, an ancient and generally accepted belief among those who had studied the ancient philosophies, ancient mysteries, and spiritual revelations. But this soul within the body did not constitute a "self" in the minds of the people in the same sense as the body did, and the soul was incapable of sin or immorality. In all of the ancient mystery teachings it was held that the soul was so closely associated with the Holy Ghost and the Holy Spirit and the breath of life that it was a divine something, an immortal, perfect thing coming into the body of man as a part of God, or of God's consciousness and kingdom, and imprisoned there with little or no opportunity to express itself except under great emotional stress or spiritual ecstasy on extreme occasions. That the spirit within man, the soul within his body, might be moved to expression at times was acknowledged and believed; and because of the mysteries that surrounded the

THE SECRET DOCTRINES OF JESUS

nature and purpose of the soul in man, the non-mystical and untrained minds believed that when the soul did express itself, it would probably do so in manners in keeping with the very mystery surrounding it. Therefore, its expressions would be in strange jerkings of the body, in weird sounds expressed through the mouth, or in a babble of words representing unknown tongues or languages, or, on certain occasions, in rhythmic motions and swayings of the body, or in the power to heal the sick, raise the dead, and perform miracles.

It was also believed that the performance of miracles and the healing of the sick were expressions of the soul that would come only to those who had developed a high degree of spiritual attunement and were messengers of God in some extreme degree. But a great many believed that when groups of human beings were assembled in spiritual seances or under the spell of spiritual stress and strain, the ecstatic state that came upon them would most easily reveal itself through the mumblings and mutterings of the soul's strange languages or the soul's peculiar control of the motions of the body. For this reason many private cults or sects grew and developed among pagan people, and even among the Jews, and we have many records of such meetings where these ex-

THE SECRET DOCTRINES OF JESUS

treme expressions of the soul constituted the ritualism of the religious service. And, strange as it may seem, such sects and cults exist today.

But only the objective, mortal self of man was qualified to be immoral or to commit sin. It was for this reason that we find in many countries unassociated systems of religious development or spiritual unfoldment in which the torture of the body constitutes the means and the method for spiritual growth. Until all the passions of the body—meaning the brain and natural senses—could be subdued, and until the inherited and acquired *instincts* of the flesh could be completely controlled, and until all of the unconscious reactions and stimuli of the physical system could be curtailed and the physical system made immune to the stimuli of nature's own worldly powers, man could not be a moral being.

As long as man was capable of reacting to worldly stimulation or reacting to the desires and urges of the flesh, of yielding to the temptations of worldly things external to his body, he was not qualified to perform his civic duties to the community. The objectionable or forbidden acts of his *mortal being* were looked upon as injurious to the community inasmuch as they constituted elements, problems, and factors that made the community unpleasant, unhappy, unhealthy, and weak in its power to fight its natural enemies and conserve its existence.

The only possible sin against the gods of the pagans and heathens was to deny the existence or the power or the possible wrath of the community god or the tribal god. Whatever else one did to a human individual was immoral because it was against the best interests of the community or contrary to one's civic duty toward the community. Lustfulness, adulterous actions, murder, theft, the practice of perversions, the appropriation of another individual's possessions or rights, the use of forbidden words, and hundreds of other acts were not classified as sins against the tribal or community god, nor as sins against the individuals concerned or involved, but against the community, the tribe, the nation.

Therefore, the code of morality was not based upon any divine commandments, divine conventions, omnipotent prohibitions, or godly proscriptions. It was a code gradually created and acknowledged and accepted by the lawmakers and rulers of the community and its dutiful citizens. Immoral behavior involved a challenge against the civic rules and regulations and brought upon the perpetrator punishment of the physical self in the hands of the citizens or those selected and authorized to fulfill the requirements of the code in that regard. Immoral and sinful acts, therefore, did not bring upon the perpetrator any divine condemnation or spiritual exclusion or critical distinction in a religious sense. If the body suffered sufficient torture and punishment for the violation of the civic code of morals, it was considered that just compensation had been made and that the sin was blotted out.

As stated above, the only exception to this was the sin against God or the gods, constituting blasphemy and a denial of the power and existence of the god or gods, in which case the perpetrator had to suffer death in order to satisfy the special requirements of the spiritual code through which the wrath of the god was expressed. Such death immediately released the soul from the body and the individual ceased to exist on earth as an individual; and therefore, as a perpetrator of a sin against God, complete annihilation of the individuality was the supreme price.

Now if we look at the moral code that Jesus referred to in so many of His parables and allegories, we see at once that there was a very great difference between His moral code and that which had been in existence for so long a time. It is true that the moral code taught by Jesus had many elements in it that were duplicates of those found in the moral code of the Jews, but still the Jews did not teach even their most learned disciples the mystical element back of the code and by virtue of which the code became truly a spiritual, moral code. In the first place, Jesus distinguishes His code of morality by making it plain to His Disciples and secret students that morality consisted of *a duty to God* and not a duty to the community. Jesus labored constantly in His public parables and allegories, preachments and actions, and in His private and secret teachings and demonstrations, to show that morality was a duty to God because it was a private matter between *a man's inner self and his God,* and that the true moral code was not a mere public matter or system, and that the chief inspiration in the moral code was not the principle of cooperation with one's fellow man or the helping of one's worldly brother, *but the saving of one's own soul.*

This moral code, as expressed by Jesus, attempted in a very subtle manner to introduce the idea that man was dual in a different sense than a *mere body of earthly elements,* and a spiritual soul imprisoned within it. He tried to establish the realization that just as man had an *outer*

THE SECRET DOCTRINES OF JESUS

self with all of its urges, sensations, and susceptibility to the influence of reasoning and thinking and of worldly impulse and temptation, so man had another self, an *inner self,* distinct from the body and only partly associated with the soul.

Despite the fact that the Christian church of modern times has laid great emphasis upon the eventual resurrection of the body and its possible entrance into the Kingdom of God, and despite the fact that certain Christian sects and denominations have so elaborated upon a mistaken conception of the idea back of the Resurrection that they hold the physical body to be holy and refuse to allow the body to be cremated—and in some cases refuse even to allow autopsies or any form of physical injury to the bones and tissue because of a belief that it would interfere with the eventual resurrection of the body and its entrance into the Kingdom of Heaven—Jesus did not teach or imply or even believe that the physical body of man was anything more than a mortal frame made of the dust of the earth and wholly unimportant in the scheme of things. This may seem shocking to many orthodox Christians, but any other viewpoint would be, and would have been, wholly inconsistent with the secret doctrines as taught and practiced by Jesus.

THE SECRET DOCTRINES OF JESUS

Nowhere in the teachings and practices of Jesus can we find the least intimation that His great system was intended to bring salvation to the *physical body of man*. Even the salvation of the soul was not taught by Jesus, and all references in the Christian Bible to the salvation of the soul constitute a misinterpretation, a misunderstanding, of the secret principle that Jesus taught. He adhered strictly, as did all of the mystics of the day and all of the mystics of the centuries preceding Him, to the fact that the soul in man was an *immortal, most perfect, divine thing,* composed of the consciousness of God, and breathed into man's physical body in order to make him "a living image of God." Wherever and whenever Jesus gave emphasis to the salvation of the spiritual, psychic part of man, it was to the third part, the *inner man,* distinct from the outer physical self and only associated temporarily with the soul while the soul was incarnate in the physical body. This inner self constituted the universal individuality, the distinct entity, the character, the perpetual self. Certainly, if the soul in man had its origin and its source in the consciousness and mind of God, it was not only immortal *but beyond contamination,* beyond sinfulness, beyond condemnation. It could, therefore, be

THE SECRET DOCTRINES OF JESUS

"saved" from nothing, and Jesus did not come to earth, nor preach and perform, suffer upon the Cross and offer His life, to "save" the soul of man.

It was because the public, the untrained and unprepared listeners, could not properly distinguish between the soul, the inner self, and the outer self that they were unable to discern the real secret message of His doctrines dealing with morals.

My reader is not to find in these words the idea that Jesus negated the idea of cooperation and the importance of each one helping his neighbor, for He taught and demonstrated the principle of each man being his brother's keeper and helper. But, more important than establishing and maintaining a civic code whose ultimate purpose and sole aim was to make a livable community, an idealistic nation, a cooperative establishment among men, was the salvation of one's inner self through a moral code that was based upon one's duty to God, to the Creator, to the Father of one's existence.

An important point in the working of this new moral code was the sacred obligation—to be taken by all who were accepted into the secret school—to renounce the world, and to develop a purely spiritual love. These two principles would enable the individual to free himself from the enslaving

THE SECRET DOCTRINES OF JESUS

powers of the world and to make himself immune to the temptations of the flesh.

The mystery schools for ages had taught that until man learns to look upon the earth and all of its offerings as a footstool kingdom intended only to serve man and not master him, and until man learns to vibrate to and express a greater degree of spiritual love than worldly or physical love, he cannot save the inner self from inevitable destruction or annihilation. The inner self, unlike the soul, is not essentially immortal save by its virtues, its morality, and its spiritual attainment. The soul in man is eternally immortal and divine. The inner man is free to choose and free to attain or be swallowed up in the fires of hell where he will be purged from association with the soul and forever separated from bodily expression.

It is the inner self as an entity that can rise in resurrection to an entrance into the Kingdom of Heaven while the physical body returns to the dust of the earth and loses its entity, its individuality, its character, and its nature.

Through the secret principles involved in the moral code proclaimed by Jesus, man's character and individuality constituting the inner self *would be saved*, and it was one's duty to God to bring into the Kingdom of Heaven, and into attunement

THE SECRET DOCTRINES OF JESUS

with His sublime presence, the inner self as an entity worthy of perpetual existence and continuous perfection.

Jesus taught secretly, and tried to reveal subtly in His parables and allegories, that it was the inner self, the character and personality within the body, that committed such sins as constituted violations of the true moral code. He taught His Disciples very privately the strange secrets of the workings of the human mind, and of the urges and impulses of the physical body, and of the erroneous reasoning and thinking of the mortal brain whereby it offered the evolving outer self temptations to sin as well as impulses to do good; but these urges and impulses and temptations were passed on to the inner self for it to decide and choose. And, in accordance with its decisions and resulting actions it had to assume the responsibility not only for its acts but for its very thoughts. Jesus made this plain in one notable instance when He explained that even to look and think lustfully and immorally toward a woman was equal to committing an immoral act.

Jesus taught that the outer physical body, with all of its mortality, could not be held responsible for its sinful acts, *since it did not possess any degree of divine consciousness or spiritual illumina-*

tion by which it could determine and decide what was evil or wrong, or what was right. It could not be made to suffer punishment at any future time, *for it had no future* but only a brief present moment of existence.

This point touches upon another one of His secret doctrines wherein He revealed to His Disciples that the physical part of man was continually changing, that the body which man had today was not the body he possessed yesterday or a year ago; that every seven hours the blood within the body was so entirely different in chemical and physical nature that it might not even be identified as the same blood; that the outer tissues of the body sloughed off constantly; that these tissues were composed of cells which died and passed out of existence; that just as the hairs of the head were constantly growing anew, so did every part of the physical body of man. He taught these facts in connection with His secret methods of healing disease and bringing about quick changes in the physical and material nature of the body and its functionings.

So the physical body of man could not be held for the sins that man committed nor could it be held to account at some future date for the sins of today, inasmuch as the body of today would not be in existence next month or next year. And, since the soul *could not commit sin* and could not therefore be held accountable for sin, it was only this evolving *inner self*, that which distinguished man from beast, that which distinguished one individual from another in characteristics of nature and in personality, that could be held responsible, and some day made accountable for the sins of man.

Another secret point in His doctrines often referred to with great emphasis by modern Christian preachers, is the idea that Jesus was the *Way* or the *Path* to man's salvation. There are two ways in which this idea is interpreted and accepted. One is the philosophical interpretation that Jesus meant that not He as an individual, but He as a *messenger*, represented the manner, the course, for right living; and that as a living example and demonstrator He became the *Way* to eternal joy and spiritual happiness. The orthodox interpretation implores us to understand that it means that we are to accept Jesus as our Saviour, our God, our Lord, our only means of salvation through His Crucifixion and through the blood He shed and through His body which suffered; that He died that we might be saved vicariously.

To the mystics of His school, however, and to those few mystics outside of His school who occasionally wandered into Palestine and listened to His parables and allegories and went back to their schools of learning to explain that a true messenger of God was on earth, the words quoted above had another meaning and one which the mystics of today accept as being the true meaning without casting aside completely the other interpretations.

Jesus meant, by intimating that He was the *Way* and the *Path,* that the revelations He was making, the unveiling of the existence within His body of a highly evolved self that was neither the physical self nor the soul, constituted a path or a means for man to discover the mystery of his own existence and afforded the opportunity for man to perfect himself and assure himself of entrance into that future Kingdom where he would be prepared and qualified to continue his spiritual evolution.

Almost every phrase uttered by Jesus, and every thought expressed by Him in allegories, parables, or definite instruction, cast light on some great mystery. Jesus Himself came among men as a mystery. To the multitudes He represented the mystery of mysteries. Even to His enemies who condemned Him and called Him a charlatan, a pretender, a false prophet, a scheming politician, and a hypocrite, He was still more than that—a mystery man. In the bottom of their hearts they

THE SECRET DOCTRINES OF JESUS

did not believe that His sole purpose in life was the charlatanism which they claimed to have found in His conduct. Neither did all of them thoroughly believe that He was only a pretender and without any power or authority. Nor did the politicians and the political rulers wholly believe that His mission in life centered exclusively around a political scheme. There was too much mystery in His acts and in His public utterances. There was entirely too much mystery in His general behavior. Then, there was the mystery of His general followers who were so numerous that the politicians could not feel safe in trusting a secret message with even the most intimate companions and associates. Then, too, there was the mystery of His strange prophecies and predictions. What did He mean, for instance, when He said that if the temple were torn down, He could rebuild it again in three days? That was not a boastful claim made unthinkingly, for Jesus had never been found making shallow and boastful claims of that kind.

That a mystery surrounded Him and surrounded His teachings and His practices is proved not only by the statements of His Disciples and Apostles and followers, and by unbiased or unprejudiced witnesses, but even by those who hated Him and those who were ready to stone Him to death, or

THE SECRET DOCTRINES OF JESUS

to hang Him upon the Cross. Even during His trial, when they stood ready with pointing fingers and attempted to charge Him with every contemptible, mean, sordid, tricky thing that the human imagination could invent, they still trembled when He moved near them and became fearful when His eyes rested on them, and whispered among themselves and in their complaints to Pilate to look out for any sudden, mysterious trick that He might perform. This is revealed to us in the manner in which Pilate called attention to Jesus standing before them near the great open window with the multitudes outside and said, "Behold, the man!" It was equivalent to saying, "Here He is, disrobed of His garments until you can see His flesh. He has no hidden arms or limbs. There He is before you denuded of all physical, all worldly mystery. Look at Him! He is just a man like yourselves; yet you have attributed to Him all the powers, all the acts, all the abilities of a superman or a monster, and then ask for His death!"

If we could have in accurate records somewhere a true and perfect picture of what His enemies thought of Him and feared in Him at the time of the trial, we would have a marvelously accurate picture of what Jesus really was, *in His inner self*. But all we have is what they said, or thought, or claimed about His *outer self,* and reverting once more, or adhering to, the ancient pagan ideas, they wanted that outer self destroyed, thinking that thereby the living entity, the living being, of this mysterious Jesus would be completely annihilated. What would become of His soul they cared nothing about. It was an immortal, divine thing like unto the souls of His enemies and His friends, and all who stood about Him. In His soul He was no different from Jew or Gentile or even the Romans whom they hated. The soul could go to the source from which it came. It was incapable of sin or immorality or pretense, hypocrisy or political scheming or anything to which they could object. It was the outer self that they thought they feared, and this they wanted destroyed that it might never again preach or teach or demonstrate the strange laws and principles which rested in that physical brain of His outer, physical body.

The *Man of Mysteries* was to become no mystery at all by the mere suffering and death of the outer self. To understand this idea is to realize the inconsistency of their point of view, and the fact that there must have been some other secret idea in His teachings regarding the triune nature of man's existence, the *body,* the *individuality within,* and the *soul.*

THE SECRET DOCTRINES OF JESUS

Herein we find the ancient, yet truly Christian, secret idea of the *trinity*.

▽

Chapter XI
THE GRAND MYSTERIES

▽

NDOUBTEDLY many of my readers will still argue that there is no good reason to believe that Jesus did not conscientiously reveal to the public every law and principle that God had implanted in His consciousness. They probably will argue that God sent His son to earth incarnated in human form and with human abilities to speak and demonstrate in order that the multitudes and all who could come within the hearing of His voice would receive all the knowledge and wisdom that the consciousness of God had stored up in the memory and understanding of Jesus. To argue that it was the sole purpose of the incarnation of Jesus on earth to *reveal* and not to *conceal*, is to forget that great truths can be destroyed by giving them common circulation and putting them in the category of everyday facts easily acquired and easily comprehended without effort or worthiness.

Casting pearls before swine has always been a sure method for not only causing many of the pearls to become lost, but for causing the swine

THE SECRET DOCTRINES OF JESUS

and all other creatures to place little value upon what is offered them. It is a tendency of human nature—and probably has been since the time of Adam and Eve—to value a thing at what it costs us to obtain or attain. That which is offered freely is worth just what it costs us to secure. To think that Jesus was unaware of this fundamental principle of human thinking, is to underestimate His marvelous knowledge of human psychology. Everything that Jesus offered the public and His Disciples was held aloft and placed in a difficult position to obtain. Even salvation, the thing that man desired the most and which Jesus offered most freely, demanded its sacrifices and its efforts. While many thought that the Way to salvation as pointed out by Jesus seemed too simple, in the face of the elaborate ritualistic requirements and devotional services of the other contemporary religions, the rich and poor alike soon found that the Christian method was the most difficult of all, and those who really wanted the spiritual purging and unfoldment and elevation that was offered to them proceeded to strive for it simply because the seemingly insurmountable difficulties made the reward appear to be something extraordinarily good.

Jesus needed leaders to carry out His mission and He knew that these men would have to be

THE SECRET DOCTRINES OF JESUS

enthusiastic, and those who placed a high value upon the trust He offered. This was why He used many methods, and especially the time-old method of carefully selecting private, secret Disciples who would become efficiently trained and who would go forth as true representatives of His divine scheme and purpose.

In answer to those who may still argue that there really were no mysteries involved in what Jesus taught and that it is an error of judgment to look upon any of His doctrines or demonstrations as real mysteries, let me say that we must remember that when the term *mysteries* is used in the New Testament and in all sacred Scripture and writings of His time and thereafter, the word *mystery* does not refer to something that is weird and seemingly incomprehensible. It refers to a secret revelation, to something that is a great truth and yet has been concealed and is still possible of understanding only by those who have become initiated or prepared and qualified, and who perhaps have been purged and cleansed and touched with the Holy Spirit to receive the special gems of truth.

We must not confound the term *mystery* with the meaning of the word as it is used in modern times, nor must we compare it with the term "magick" of ancient times.

THE SECRET DOCTRINES OF JESUS

Jesus could not have interested the multitudes, let alone the learned ones, in any new system of magical mysteries or tricks. Today the modern world looks with astonishment upon the professional performances of magic and legerdemain as not only something highly entertaining, but truly mysterious and *almost* supernatural. But even the greatest of the puzzling and mysterious tricks of the modern magician would have been smiled at, and even scoffed at, by the learned ones and by the general public of the times of Jesus' mission on earth. Both Egypt and India and other lands in the Near East and Far East were accustomed to mysterious performances, to manifestations of so-called "white magick," to such a degree that the adepts who still perpetuate those mysteries in modern times astonish and perplex the masterful scientific magicians of today.

With all of our so-called scientific miracles that we think would have astonished and even frightened the people of ancient times, we cannot duplicate, in a professional trickster's manner, the feats of natural law and divine law which were commonly demonstrated in the years immediately preceding the birth of Jesus. Even the raising of the dead was not an uncommon or surprising thing prior to the birth of Jesus, and if

THE SECRET DOCTRINES OF JESUS

He had attempted to win the multitudes to His doctrines or His religious, divine system solely through the raising of the dead or the healing of the blind and the lame, He would have succeeded to no greater degree than did others before Him.

The mysteries which Jesus dealt with were of a transcendental nature and revealed divine principles and a special power to perform, which the students of the ancient wisdoms and spiritual revelations had always understood as existing in some being somewhere, or as potential with God and probably transferable to an avatar or divine messenger of some unique qualifications, but undemonstrated and untaught to more than a secret few.

When Jesus said to those whom He trusted and was preparing, "I come to show you a mystery," He meant something far different than anything that they had seen or heard about in past years, and we, today, who are attempting to fathom these mysteries and to glimpse even a small portion of the power and transcendental magnificence of them, keenly realize that the mysteries which Jesus taught so secretly and demonstrated so guardedly are indeed worthy of continued protection from the profane eyes and minds of the curious public.

THE SECRET DOCTRINES OF JESUS

We not only believe that these great secrets have been carefully preserved and are susceptible of understanding and repeated performance, but we believe that even greater things can be accomplished through the same principles which He taught, but that the student and practitioner must be found worthy and must be bound to secrecy and must attain true discipleship.

This need for careful selection is emphasized in so many passages of the New Testament that it is absurd to assert that the analytical student of Christian doctrines or the careful reader of the Christian Bible can believe that the Christian church of today and all of its representatives are familiar with the real secret doctrines and real mysteries represented by the secret school of Jesus.

The Jews of His time recognized the fact that what Jesus was teaching and demonstrating was not the result of simple intellectual comprehension and attainment. We must continually bear in mind that He was carefully observed by the most learned of the Jews and His doctrines were torn to shreds by the keen minds of those who wanted to discover in them some taint of common mystical philosophy. Not only did He surprise His elders with His profound knowledge of matters that were generally unknown to young people or even to

THE SECRET DOCTRINES OF JESUS

learned people, but His discerning mind and very evident attunement with the Divine Consciousness made it possible for Him to solve the most difficult of theological, philosophical, moral, and ethical problems.

Take the occasion, for instance, when He went up into the Temple and taught for a number of days. In the 15th verse of the seventh chapter of the Book of John we are told that the Jews wondered at His marvelous teachings saying, "How knoweth this man the Scriptures, having never learned them?" They referred to the fact that even the most superficially trained of their learned men had to spend half a lifetime not only in deep and profound meditation and analysis over the holy writings of the past, but in memorizing them and in examining each and every thought and idea from every possible angle and being able to answer hundreds of questions directed from every point of view on each and every principle. And we are told in that same chapter that Jesus answered them and said, "My teaching is not mine, but His that sent me."

Over and over again Jesus frankly and modestly explained that the things He taught and the things He did were not the result of the prowess of His own intellect, but the result of divine inspiration

THE SECRET DOCTRINES OF JESUS

and divine revelation and of a special preparedness that constituted a divine messiahship.

Let us take another example of His secret way of dealing with these matters. In the fourth chapter of the Book of Mark we have an interesting story of the public teachings of Jesus with parables and symbols, allegories, and veiled phrases, and then in the 10th verse we read that, "When He was alone, they that were about Him, with the Twelve, asked of Him the parables. And He said unto them, 'To you is given the mystery of the Kingdom of God; but unto them that are without, all things are done in parables.'"

A careful reading of the entire story shows us that the multitude stood about and listened to a large number of His parables, and when He apparently was through His period of teaching for the day, the multitude passed on, whispering among themselves and asking one another what it was all about, and whether He was to be relied upon, and whether some of His remarks were meant sarcastically for some of them or directed toward certain others in the country, and, perhaps, meant to be critical of their religious beliefs. The scoffers and the half-believers along with the evil-minded ones and the self-satisfied ones passed on, gaining little or nothing from the parables they

THE SECRET DOCTRINES OF JESUS

had heard. Today we find duplicates of that early picture!

We are told that when He finally found Himself alone there were those about Him, *including the Twelve,* who began to ask Him questions about the parables He had just used. These words of the 10th verse clearly indicate that there were two groups or two kinds of persons present when He considered Himself as being "alone." There was the large circle of interested, believing listeners, and the smaller circle, constituting the twelve Apostles. This gives another picture of the hundred and twenty Disciples or students of the secret school with the twelve Apostles as counselors and leaders. We understand now why Jesus answered them and said that to those in front of Him and about Him in this secret group of one hundred and twenty it was written or decreed that eventually they should know "the secrets" of the Kingdom of God while to those without—to those who were without the pale of discipleship in His secret student body, those who represented the outer worldly circle of ordinary passers-by—all would be revealed only in parables.

His Disciples had seen so many of the mysteries demonstrated that they never questioned His explanations even though many of these apparently

THE SECRET DOCTRINES OF JESUS

contradicted the scientific thought of the day. Still, even some of the mystery schools of this very period in the twentieth century are teaching and demonstrating laws and principles that prove themselves to be contrary to the theoretical postulations of science. The attempt to reduce all of the miracles of the Bible and all the mysteries of life to simple, natural, scientific theorems is rapidly proving unsatisfactory to thinking minds.

Let us take, for example, occurrences during the great World War [I]. Thousands of mothers in various parts of the world had experiences which proved to them beyond all scientific argument or learned protests that time and space do not exist in the world of spirit and that the consciousness of a human being can project itself through space and make itself objectively sensed to those held in mind by the one who is thus extending the real self into the distance.

Recalling the fact that Jesus was secretly teaching the existence of an inner self that was independent of the outer physical self and strangely related to the soul, Jesus proved His contention in this regard by actual demonstrations. On more than one occasion He appeared in their midst while in every physical, material sense, His body and mind, as well as His soul, were at a distant point.

THE SECRET DOCTRINES OF JESUS

His Disciples were not surprised, therefore, but rather anticipated the experience when Jesus appeared in the closed room after His Resurrection. The Holy Scriptures of the New Testament make it plain that they were assembled secretly in a closed room *through which no physical body could have entered,* yet Jesus appeared there not as by stepping from one room into another, but gradually, in a visible form right in their very midst.

The thought conveyed in the record of this event is that the spiritual self that appeared in their very midst grew in substance or in visible quality before their very eyes as though a mystic cloud gradually became more dense and more definite in form and finally took on the objective aspect and conditions of a physical body. And to prove that this was no mere apparition, He showed to them that it was in fact a projection of the physical form, the spiritual consciousness, of His body, for there were the holes in the hands and the feet and the scars upon the brow and the wound in the side. If this appearance had been solely a "soul-projection" or a "spiritual projection of the soul" as modern *spiritualists* ask us to understand and accept, the wounds in His fleshly body would not have been apparent, for we cannot reverse all of our understanding of these fundamentals and believe that a wound in the flesh and tissue of the physical body creates or causes an accompanying injury to the soul.

And, there was the secret formula that was given so definitely to those who understood and which was interpreted merely as an allegorical statement by those who were outside of the secret circle. He had told them not only how the consciousness could be projected to a distant point and made visible, but how each of them could call upon the inner self of a distant being and bring it to their presence or so attune themselves with the distant self that gradually that distant self would become visible or tangible in the very room or presence of the one or more who called upon the self.

We know today that to understand this great mystery of projection of consciousness and projection of self—or to take the first step in this mystical process—necessitates the mastery of many carefully prepared lessons dealing with fundamental divine and natural laws. There are those today who practice this process with reverence as well as profound intellectual understanding, and who know that it is not the result of the violation of any natural law as many would suspect, but the application of natural law with divine

THE SECRET DOCTRINES OF JESUS

understanding along with the application of truly divine principles.

In giving the formula to His Disciples in an allegorical manner, He associated it with praying because the formula by which a projection from a distant point is called forth, or the self prepares to extend its consciousness to a distant point, is like unto the utterance of a petition. So Jesus told them that when they prayed and wanted to sense attainment in their prayers and be one with Him again in body and spirit as He explained at the Last Supper, they should pray in His name and that wherever two or more of them came together, in privacy and in isolation from the hubbub of worldly affairs, and prayed "in His name" or called upon Him with the mystical formula, there He would be in their midst.

The doing of things and the saying of things, and the praying for things "in His name" did not mean what it is generally interpreted as meaning. Every student of ancient and Christian mystical principles understands very definitely what is meant in a formula by "in His name." In the name of the Christus, in the name of the Christ, in the name of the Holy Ghost or the Holy Spirit, in the name of the Holy Trinity, in the name of the Logos, the great Amen, represents a very definite formula practiced by Jesus and His Disciples and privately practiced today by the secret schools of the ancient wisdom. The explanation of all this and the practice of the principles whereby the secret students prepared and qualified themselves to go forth into the world and make themselves visible here and there, and to enter places through closed doors and closed windows, or through the walls of mud and stone, or through the bars of iron or steel, constitutes another one of the great secret doctrines.

The turning of water into wine, the feeding of the bread to the multitudes, the transmutation of grosser things into finer things, the alchemy of the spirit, the development of the power of faith, the increasing of the human aura whereby the spiritual and divine radiations of the God consciousness within would heal and cure, were others of the secret doctrines which have been preserved, not only in the old and musty archives of the crypts of the early Christian churches, but in the practical and mystical teachings of the secret schools of today which represent the Great White Brotherhood.

All of the secret schools today which are classified as *initiatic* (because the students within them must first be prepared and made ready, and then

THE SECRET DOCTRINES OF JESUS

spiritually and *esoterically initiated* before receiving the Truth) are associated in one secret organization or federation for the exchange of helpful suggestions and ideas relating to the ways and means not only of perpetuating the secret doctrines which Jesus taught but the manner of selecting the final Disciples and Apostles who shall go forth, not to destroy the faith and religions of the world, but to carry out the great mission for which Jesus was preordained and predestined to become a Son of God incarnate.

Whether or not the Christian churches and Christian followers under their great leaders accept these ideas and perceive the truth concealed in this book is immaterial to the success of the Great Work that is being carried on by the perpetuators and conservators of the divine ordination. They carry no sword and brandish no flame of fire, but in peace and secret contentment devote their lives to the dissemination of knowledge to those who are worthy. Their outer form of propaganda is no more boastful, no more bombastic or radical, than the propaganda carried on by Jesus Himself when He rose up on the heights of the rocks or mountains and looking over the multitudes assembled, proclaimed the coming of a new kingdom, the coming of a heaven to earth, the self-condem-

THE SECRET DOCTRINES OF JESUS

nation of the sinful, the salvation of those who followed on the Path and who accepted Him as "The Way" to eternal life.

These secret teachers and leaders constitute a hierarchy governing an enormous invisible empire whose existence is little suspected by the scoffers, the doubters, the self-satisfied. They claim no unique birth and no supernatural powers. They repeat only the old, old assertion that they are *Messengers of Light* bringing to earth the message of Him who inspired them and carrying out in fact the work of the Holy Ghost that came upon their ancestors at the time that Jesus breathed upon them and asked God to ordain them.

They still speak in parables and allegories to the public and call attention to their great mission by every means available just as Jesus did. They suffer the rebukes and condemnation of the multitudes and the physical and material punishments of the enemies of Light. Yet their followers increase in numbers, they abide in peace and happiness, they grow in wisdom and the Holy Spirit, and represent today the true brotherhood of man working for the establishment on earth of the Kingdom of God. Through books and pamphlets and the voice of the radio, through public assemblies and private discourses, they open the

THE SECRET DOCTRINES OF JESUS

portals to those who are sincere; and between the lines of their messages in whatever form delivered, they reveal as through a veil the simple outline of truths which the seeker is invited to investigate; and when the student believes himself ready, or by his inquiring attitude and open-mindedness reveals he is ready, the *master teacher* will appear and the *Way* will be made plain.

CHAPTER XII

PROGRESSIVE MODIFICATIONS OF THE CHRISTIAN DOCTRINES

▽

IN RECENT years we have heard much about revisions, alterations, modifications and eliminations in Christian church rituals, doctrines and rules; but we may not realize that this process of alteration and modification has been in operation since the first century after the passing of the Keys to Saint Peter, and that the process has always extended itself to include the fundamental *doctrines* of Christ's teachings and the teachings of His official disciples.

In fact, very few of the essential, fundamental doctrines of the original Christian sect have come down to us in their pristine purity.

The so-called *fundamentalists,* who claim that they are endeavoring to *retain* the fundamentals of Christianity, and protect the religion against the intrusions of modern thought or the modifications of liberal thinkers, know little indeed as to what was fundamental and what is an invention of later centuries. That which most of them are striving

THE SECRET DOCTRINES OF JESUS

to retain in its "pure form" is very far from being truly Christian in spirit or form.

In every century since the actual establishment of the Christian church, there have been so-called *fundamentalists* protesting against any modifications, and insisting upon the rigid obedience to certain doctrines and principles which they claimed were "original" and pure. Yet, most of the principles and doctrines thus classified, were of council decree or arbitrary invention. For instance, what were being protected in the eighth century A.D., by the *fundamentalists*, as the original dictums of Christ were, in many instances, inventions and arbitrary decrees of the Church Fathers and high councils of the preceding century.

The *fundamentalists* of today are striving to protect doctrines and principles which have been created, invented or arbitrarily adopted in scores of ecclesiastical councils and "official decrees" in the past eight hundred years.

Take, for instance, the doctrine of the "Holy Trinity." It is looked upon by the *fundamentalists* as one of the original and most sacred of Christian essentials. Yet it was not until the 12th century A.D. that the Church Fathers in a Lateran Council, discussed the formation—actual invention of the *Trinity* in more or less its present form, adopted it, and proclaimed it as a *fundamental!*

It is true that in a mystical sense the *sacred triangle* was part of the secret symbolism of the original Christian sect, during the lifetime of Christ; and it had been a sacred symbol for centuries before the birth of Christ; and is still a sacred symbol of a very great and essential doctrine of many mystical religions. It was a symbol of the "mysteries" to which Jesus often referred, and which were never revealed to the outer circle of Christian followers. But, the doctrine of the *Trinity*, as we have it today (with many additions and modifications in spirit) was not known to or adopted by the Christian *church* until the 12th century, and it has little resemblance to the ancient mystical understanding of the symbolism of the sacred triangle.

The Christian religion of today—and for the past five centuries—is filled, in its doctrines, ritualism, rules, and conduct, with liberal extractions from *paganism*. This may seem like a shocking statement to most sincere Christians, and should be illuminating to those *fundamentalists* who insist that there shall be no divergences from the pristine teachings of Jesus.

As an example or two, consider the very important, sacred and *"fundamentally pure"* holy day known as Easter. If it were the anniversary of an historical event, as *Christmas Day* is supposed to be, it should fall on the same date each year. But, its date is movable, and is determined each year by astrological or astronomical occurrences, in accordance with the very old pagan system. In fact Easter Day is so old a pagan holiday—of purely mystical and mythological meaning—that its origin is lost. As for Christmas Day—the day of the birth of Jesus the Christ—the early Christian church used many dates for this sacred celebration and there was constant dispute during the first five centuries as to what date in December, January, and even February, should be officially decreed as the actual date of birth of our Lord Jesus. Finally an old, very old, pagan holiday was adopted—that of a mythological and mystical nature—falling on December twenty-fifth.

Nearly all of the dates of Christian Holy Days have been fixed upon ancient pagan holy days, with new, original and purely arbitrary interpretations. Very few of them have any relation to, or foundation in, any of the doctrines, teachings or practices of Jesus during His lifetime, or during the lifetime of any of His original Disciples.

In reading the carefully recorded discussions of the Christian Councils of the third, fourth, fifth

THE SECRET DOCTRINES OF JESUS

and following centuries, one is continually impressed with the arbitrary stand taken by many of the Councilors, and the ingenuity of the Council's vote. The admitted policy of "ecclesiastical necessity" seems to have been the sole rule and guide by which doctrines, principles of ritual and practice were rejected, modified, altered, and—blandly invented.

Not the pure mystical or spiritual interpretation of the teachings of Jesus, not that which would unfold and unveil His sacred principles, determined what should or should not be added or eliminated from the mass of traditional matter under consideration, but what would build the Church as a *physical organization* to greater size and power, and what would most *conveniently* meet the needs of *churchianity*, were given sole consideration. A very definite distinction must be made between Christianity and Churchianity, in considering the evolution of the Christian religion. Today, everything *in* and *of* the Christian religion is subservient to *churchianity*. Is it any wonder that the mystical spirit, the mystical doctrines and practices of the original Christian sect are almost wholly unknown to the general membership of the worldwide Christian church—either Roman Catholic or Protestant?

THE SECRET DOCTRINES OF JESUS

It is generally conceded by conscientious authorities within the Christian church that many of the present-day doctrines and teachings were *invented* or extracted from pagan religions, solely because of "ecclesiastical necessity" or "expediency."

Take for example the fundamental doctrine of the *original sin*. For the Church to have held, simply, that all men must be saved or redeemed from the sins of their own commission, and of which they were guilty, would have eliminated the necessity of redeeming those who had lived a good and sinless life—and particularly millions of infants and little children who had never committed an actual sin or any act of which they were "guilty."

To increase the membership of the Church, to build it greater and greater in a purely physical form, all mankind, of every religious belief, of every age—even infants and children—*must* find redemption and salvation, *exclusively in the Christian church!* The most Godly of beings, the most holy of little children, must be forced into the Church to be saved—from what? It was not enough that only those should be saved who had knowingly or unknowingly committed one or more of the increasing number of sins listed by the

THE SECRET DOCTRINES OF JESUS

Church; every living creature, even those created and born in the Image of God, and of goodly acts, must be saved and redeemed.

As an "ecclesiastical necessity" the doctrine of the *original sin* was created, invented out of whole cloth, and officially decreed as a very fundamental principle. No matter how short an earthly life one might have lived—even a brief hour—nor how perfectly and in what a Godly manner might one have lived, one was still cursed with the sin by *inheriting the original sin*. From that inheritance none could escape—not even the little babe whose soul was just projected from the Divine Consciousness of God!

The doctrine was truly a "necessity"! It has proved to be the most objectionable of all to millions of thinking men and women, and especially to parents who hold in their arms, for the first time, a little babe in all its certain goodness.

Yet, we are told that God is a God of Justice, Mercy, and Love! Still, the innocent must inherit, through the *Will of God*, a sin that condemns the soul to everlasting punishment—unless it is redeemed.

Nowhere, in the original teachings of Jesus, do we find this doctrine represented as the Church represents it. It is the most conspicuous of the

THE SECRET DOCTRINES OF JESUS

many inconsistent, contradictory doctrines of the Christian religion of today.

The Christian religion—the Christian form of *churchianity*—is one of the most complex systems of today, as compared with the extreme and magnificent simplicity of the *system* unfolded by Jesus. During His lifetime His followers—and bitter critics—made much of the fact that His *system of salvation,* His Way, was so simple to comprehend, so direct and logical, and so easy for the sincere to adopt and follow, that it was either manifestly *divine,* or *ridiculously childish,* according to the mind of the commentator.

Before Jesus outlined His simple doctrines and revealed the straight and narrow *Path,* the people to whom He preached had battled with complexities and involved procedures in religion, to a point where none but the High Priests understood all of the principles, all of the laws, all of the rituals, and all of the prescribed and proscribed practices. In the so-called pagan religions there were a multiplicity of *gods,* an endless number of "symbolical indulgences" and a continuous flow of new and arbitrary rulings, doctrines, and interpretations. In the religion of Israel, the ritualism, doctrines, and practices had become so involved that a lifetime of study was necessary to find the perfect code of life.

THE SECRET DOCTRINES OF JESUS

As a great flash of lightning dispels the darkness, so the astonishing, yet simple, statements of Jesus, revealed the fundamentals of God's laws. "Love thy neighbor; become as a child; do unto others as you would have them do unto you; abandon the vain-glorious things of the world; seek the Kingdom of Heaven *within;* lift up your consciousness to God in prayer and communion," and other easily understood rules, constituted the true Path to Eternal Life.

Today we find in the Christian church a similar multiplicity of *gods*—called *Saints*—with a constantly increasing number of new and modified doctrines, rules, and practices. In the matter of *prayer* and *divine communion,* instead of the simple instructions of Jesus to pray *directly* and *privately* to "Our Father who art in Heaven," we find the present-day *system* of prayer an involved ritualistic program, with instructions to direct our prayers to a large number of Saints as mediators. The injunction, "Thou shalt have no other Gods before me!" is lost sight of in the complexity of ritualism; and the sublime, mystical privilege of direct communion with God is discouraged by the ponderous system of *churchianity*.

At this very hour—and every hour of each passing year—somewhere in the numerous groups of

THE SECRET DOCTRINES OF JESUS

Christian sectarian divisions, there are individuals or small committees and councils of Church leaders, debating the addition to or modification of the Christian doctrines, and laboriously struggling to give newer and more modern interpretations to the simple *truths*—unalterable truths—spoken by Jesus to His Disciples.

The Christian religion in its present-day *popular* form is no longer the divinely inspired religion of Jesus, but a man-made system of pagan and modern ideas carefully fabricated to *conceal*, rather than *reveal*, the transcendental jewels in the diadem of pristine teachings of Jesus the Christ.

▽

CHAPTER XIII

THE PRESERVATION OF THE SECRET TEACHINGS

▽

NOTHING said in the preceding chapter should imply that in the passing of the centuries the original and pure teachings of Jesus have been lost to the world, or that His secret doctrines, practices, and methods are no longer known to man; nor should it be thought that the continuous modification, alteration, interpretation, and invention of so many new and inconsistent principles have obscured forever the truth He taught in His secret school.

Unquestionably the Holy Roman Church has preserved in its secret archives in Rome—or elsewhere—many sacred manuscripts that contain the essential teachings of Jesus in their earliest and almost pure form. There is considerable evidence to indicate that within its sealed vaults, inaccessible to all but a very few, are certain original documents written and signed during the lifetime of Jesus. Some other rare documents preserved in the Vatican—or within the walls of Vatican City—are copies of original documents and records which are preserved in archives, outside of the control of the Holy Roman Church.

In other places, fortified archives of great antiquity, are preserved other documents and records; and in the secret archives of several monastic orders of a non-sectarian nature are preserved, and open to occasional examination by competent authorities, the manuscripts of persons, mostly reliable witnesses, living during the years of the ministry of Jesus.

From all of these it is possible to gather facts that shed much light on the life and teachings of Jesus, and especially on the *truths* which Jesus taught in His secret school.

To believe that the creators of the Holy Roman Church made no exhaustive study of the manuscripts and records in their possession, or which they had agents searching for in every land, is to ignore the fact that their own records of their Council discussions and debates reveal how carefully they weighed every reference to the doctrines, teachings, demonstrations, and practices of Jesus and His Disciples. For days at a time they tore to shreds every sacred principle, every precept, every quoted phrase, of the teachings of Jesus, and every performance or application of His mystical power. Every thought and act was

THE SECRET DOCTRINES OF JESUS

weighed in the balance. Unless each fitted, like a link in a chain, in the *system of theology* they were creating, it was either rejected or "officially interpreted." Where links were missing or "incompatible," new links were invented.

Year after year, century after century, these debates continued, and the records of them clearly show that the Councilors had before them many rare records which they officially proclaimed as either "incompetent," dangerous, secret, or contradictory to the principles of Christian theology which they were gradually establishing.

Reference has already been made in the "Mystical Life of Jesus" to the many alterations that were made, during the course of many years, in the so-called "Apostles' Creed." The discussions on this great subject reveal that the fathers of the slowly evolving Roman Church had before them many rare records of the true Christian teachings, as well as reliable records of what actually occurred during the Crucifixion, "burial," and Ascension of Jesus. But, the real facts were deliberately concealed.

The matter of the selection of the manuscripts constituting the "Books of the Bible" offers an excellent picture of how these *high councils* arbitrarily chose and rejected authentic and reliable sources of information at their disposal. The re-

THE SECRET DOCTRINES OF JESUS

ports of *why* certain admittedly genuine manuscripts were rejected, and others which are still shrouded in mystery and doubt, were finally voted upon as being the only ones to constitute the *official* Bible, cast much light on the point as to whether the original teachings of Jesus and His Disciples were preserved after the Ascension of Jesus.

But it is not only in the sealed archives of the Vatican, nor in the archives of old monastic orders, that the secrets of the school of Jesus were preserved.

While the Christian Bible says much of the missionary work of the principal Disciples—the leaders of the twelve groups of carefully trained students in the secret school of Jesus—little or nothing is said of the work of these hundred or more secret workers.

It is inconceivable that Jesus should have gone to such great lengths to establish and maintain, even at the cost of life and liberty, such an institution, and to have devoted hours of the days and nights, for years, to preparing the carefully selected and tried adepts, with no plan or program for the future.

Certainly, if there were a plan—a scheme for *The Great Work*—it must have been predicated

THE SECRET DOCTRINES OF JESUS

upon the necessity of continuing His institution—call it a *church, school,* or *order*—after His retirement. (Even the Christian Bible, as well as many other sacred records, reports the many occasions when Jesus plainly intimated that His earthly efforts would be cut short while still in the prime of life. Therefore, He must have made some provision for the continuance of the work which He had established. Twelve men—the Apostles—alone could not have accomplished, after His "crucifixion," what required over one hundred and twenty men and women during His active leadership.)

It is absurd to think that the trial, crucifixion, burial, and ascension brought a complete end to His secret plans and elaborate institution. What became of the hundred or more tried, tested, and truly prepared adepts? Could Jesus have selected such weaklings, such insincere and easily discouraged members of His secret school as would have lost all interest, forgotten all their pledges, and abandoned all their power—divinely bestowed upon them on one momentous occasion—just because their leader had been persecuted? Men and women do not easily forsake a divine gift, a divine heritage, that enables them to shed Light, Life, and Love among the multitudes. There is

THE SECRET DOCTRINES OF JESUS

ample evidence to prove that His hundred or more adepts continued to meet, to hold secret sessions of the school, to initiate new recruits, and to carry the work into lands far beyond the horizon of Palestine. Records in many countries bordering on the Mediterranean, and as far north as China, show that these original adepts and their successors visited these lands and established branches of the *Great School,* always carrying on the missionary work in the form of a larger outer circle of general students or seekers, and an *inner circle* of initiated adepts.

Naturally the necessity for preserving the *truths* which Jesus taught, and especially of *conserving* in their pristine form the divine formulae which Jesus used and secretly demonstrated in His performance of miracles and the "mysteries," caused them to be recorded in permanent form in symbols, ciphers, and signs. By word of mouth and by personal instruction only, behind closed and tiled doors, were these things transmitted from initiator to the initiated, year after year, and century after century.

Under various symbolical names, the branches of The Great School continued through the ages. The Great School was little concerned with the later establishment of a *sectarian church* claiming

THE SECRET DOCTRINES OF JESUS

to be wholly and purely Christian and yet differing in its doctrines from those taught by Jesus. The Great School had no interest in the building of huge edifices for worship, the creation of elaborate ritualism for public assemblies, or the invention of theological systems constituting *churchianity*. The *path* which Jesus pointed out was to be followed by each individual in privacy and silence. Salvation, spiritual development, and divine attunement were personal, individual qualities, not collective or group attainments.

It was inevitable that a wide separation should come between the adepts and followers of The Great School, and the movement known as the *Christian church*. The latter was continuously adopting and developing features that made it a rival of the pagan and Jewish religions; the Great School ever remained the Invisible Kingdom of Heaven on earth.

Down through the ages the work of the Great School continued. It took various forms such as secret assemblies, monastic orders, and concealed fraternities, adapting its operations to the necessities, limitations, and specific conditions of time and place.

Several outer forms of organizations were gradually established to *conserve* and *propagate* the secret teachings of Jesus. One of these was the *Order of the Rosy Cross* (the Rosicrucian Order) in whose charge was placed the preservation and practice of the scientific, spiritual, and divine formulae of the Great School. Another was the semi-monastic order of Martinism (the Martinist Order) in whose charge was placed the preservation, practice, and teachings of some of the purely religious teachings of Jesus the Christ.

Today, throughout the world, these two organizations—operating under slightly different variations of name to conform to the linguistic and other distinctions of each country, but adhering to the ancient rules and dictums of the international council of the *Great White Brotherhood*—are carrying on the unaltered purposes of the secret school established by Jesus. Neither of the organizations constitutes a *church* in the sense generally applied to that word in these modern times, nor do they seek to supplant the established churches of any creed or land. Their work is that of *supplementing* the work of all churches and religious movements by teaching and establishing those doctrines, truths, and eternal principles which have been eliminated from, or modified in the arbitrarily made systems of religion existing throughout the universe.

THE SECRET DOCTRINES OF JESUS

In the inner circles of the Rosicrucian Brotherhood are to be found the Holy Assemblies that gave such spiritual strength and power to the original Great School. Those who seek to know the mysteries of man and man's life here, heretofore, and hereafter, on earth, will find them—gradually and by being worthy—in the Order of the Rosicrucians. Those who seek to know the mysteries of the divine revelations of Jesus in His original and Christly Way, will find them through preparation and guidance in the circle of the Martinist Order. This organization has its central, world headquarters in Europe, with chartered branches and active organizations in various parts of the world. In the United States is located the Grand Regional Collegium and Council of the Martinist Order for North America. It can be approached only by being ready and being invited in due time.

▽

INDEX

▽

A

Acts, Book of: 154-155; 164
  Quote, 139, 162-163
Advisory Council, 99, 110, 114
Akhenaten, (See Amenhotep IV)
Amenhotep IV: 69
  Conflicts, 40-41
  Monotheism, 41, 69
Andrew, St., 155
Apostles: 28, 58
  Advisory Council, 99, 110, 114, 132
  After Crucifixion, 137-140; 229
  Creed, 227
  Holy Ghost, 140, 141, 147
  Remission of sins, 143-145
  Secret Teachings, 204-211
Aramaic language, 91-93
Ascension, 36, 146-147; 167, 227-228; 229
Aura, 210
Avatars:
  Pre-Christian, 64-67

B

Bartholomew, 155
Bethany, 110
Bible:
  Books, 227
  King James version, 153
  Misinterpretations, 17-22
  Synoptic Gospels, 25, 153
  Verification, 149-172
  (See also New Testament, Old Testament, Acts, John, Mark, Luke, Matthew)
Black Magic, 123
Blood, 118-119; 139-140
Book of the Dead, 138
Bread, Symbol, 118, 139
Breathing on Disciples, 140-141
Brothers and Sisters: 160-162
  Disciples, 19, 55-56; 162-163
Brown, Rev. David, 83

C

Catholic Church, Holy Roman:
  Failures of, 79
  Fathers, 76-77
  Secret Archives, 37, 76, 225-226; 228
  System of theology, 216-228
China, 230
Christian and Christianity:
  Councils, 216, 218-219
  Early leaders, 36
  Fellowship, 133
  Saints, 63-64; 223
  View of other teachings, 74
  Vs. paganism, 177-183
  Workers, 24
  (See also Christian Church; Disciples)
Christian Church:
  Apostles' Creed, 227
  Children, 220-221
  Christmas Day, 218
  Churchianity, 219, 222-224
  Communion, 223
  Easter, 218
  Failures, 21, 25, 29-31; 79-81
  Fathers, 76-77
  Fundamentalists, 215-217
  Gods of, 223

[234]

Keys to, 36-37; 39, 215
Needs, 30-31; 202
Original sin, 220-221
Pagan-Jewish extractions,
  217-219; 231
Prayer, 223
Remission of sin, 142-143
Resurrection of body,
  185-186; 189-191
Trinity, 216-217
Women, 156
(See also Catholic Church)
Christian Science, 130
Christmas Day, 218
Church,
  (See Christian Church)
Communion,
  (See Divine Communion)
Cosmic:
  Course, 167
  Principles, 24, 58
  Revelations, 40, 43
Council of Sanhedrin, 167
Cross, 57-59; 109, 134, 194
  Symbol of, 86
Crucifixion: 134, 157, 166-167; 227-229
  Fulfillment, 58-59; 109
  Prophecy, 57
Cults, 100-101

D

Devils:
  Ancient, 124-127
  Cast out, 135
  Today, 128-132
Disciples:
  After Crucifixion, 137,
    171-172; 228-230
  Baptism, 113
  Brothers and Sisters, 19, 55
  Crucifixion, 58-59
  Mary, 18-20; 55, 158-160
  Missions, 97-105
  Modern Christianity, 63-64
  New Testament, 81-82
  Number, 170-171
  Prayer and Faith, 131-132
  Promised perfection, 56-58
  Purpose, 77
  Reasons for secrecy,
    170-171
  Secret society, 26-29
  Secret teachings, 36-37; 39
  Selection, 26-28; 49, 199
  Twelve (See Apostles)
Divine:
  Birth, 25-26
  Communion, 223
  Conception, 62
  Consciousness, 78
  Diploma, 108
  Illumination, 41-45
  Principles, 122-123
Documents, 226

E

Easter, 218
Education, Illumination,
  41-45
Egypt:
  Magic demonstrations, 200
  Religion, 61
  Secret schools, 39
  Teachings of, 74
Essenes, 29

F

Faith, 103-104; 131, 210
Fall of man, 178
Fausset, Rev. A. R., 83
Fishermen, 91-93
Freemasons, 31
Fundamentalists, 215-217

G

Galilee, 111
Glastonbury, 169
God: 34-35; 52
  Attunement, 53
  Consciousness, 78
  Soul, 179-183; 185-188
  Universal laws, 53
Golgotha, 59
Grail, 117-118
Great Britain, 169
Great White Brotherhood,
  210-233

H

Hell, 136
Hermeticists, 31
Hindu, religion, 61
Holy Ghost: 71-72; 199, 209
  Disciples, 57, 139-141; 144-147
  Jesus, 41
  Soul, 179

I

Immaculate Conception, 62
Immortality, doctrine, 133-134
India:
  Magic demonstrations, 200
  Secret Schools, 39, 74
Initiation, 84-96; 211
  (See also Disciples)

J

James, Judas, 155
Jamison, Rev. Robert, 83
Jerusalem, 115
Jesus:
  Atonement, the, 71
  Betrayal, 109, 164-167
  Burial, 136, 227-229
  Crucifixion, 57-59
  Early life, 41-45; 98
  His teachings, 45-48; 113-114
  Last Supper, 209-210
  Meetings, 51-55
  Mission, 67-72; 97-105
  Mother (See Mary)
  On the Cross, 134-136
  Power, 123
  Purification, 108-109; 114
  Resurrection, 137-139; 146, 157, 166-167; 207
  Secret followers, 48-50
  (See also Disciples: Secret Teachings, etc.)
Jews and Jewish:
  Antagonism toward Jesus, 108-109; 113-114; 192-195
  Jesus in Temple, 203
  Language, 91-92
  Passover, 114
  Religion, 68
John the Baptist, 113
John, St.: 115, 155
  Quote, 140, 161-162; 203
Jordan River, 98
Joseph, Barsabas, 166
Joseph of Arimathea, 136, 166-170
Judas: 109, 138, 164-165
  Brother James, 155
Judgment of sinners, 144-145

K

Karma, 141-146

L

Logos, 209
Luke: 163, 167
  Quote, 122, 124

M

Magicians, 125-127
Mark, St., 64, 121, 167, 204
Martinists, 232-233
Mary: 155 (See Disciples)
  Student of Jesus, 18-20
Matthew, St.: 63-64; 121, 155
  Quote, 122, 160-161
Meetings, 27, 51-55
Messengers of Light, 212
Messiah, Jewish, 68
Miracles:
  Greatest, 133-147
  Pagan, 180
Mission, 67-72; 97-98
Moral code:
  Jesus, 176-177; 183-185
  Pagan, 177-183
Mount of Olives, 154
Mysteries, 82-85; 197-201
  (See also Secret Teachings)
Mystic Circle, 59
Mystical Life of Jesus, The, 44, 62, 150, 154, 227

P

Pagan and Paganism:
  Christians, 217-219
  Gods, 222
  Magicians, 125-128
  Moral Codes, 177-185
  Superstitions, 125
Palestine:
  Cults, 45-47, 100-101
  Religious movements, 156
Parables:
  Concealed truths, 29, 204-205
  Dual meanings, 91-95
  Egyptian, 85
  Inner self, 189
  Moral code, 183
  Purpose, 86, 90-91
Persia, 39, 74
Peter, 36, 37, 115, 155, 215
Philip, 155
Philosophers, ancient, 64-67
Photographs:
  Church of Nativity
  Garden Tomb of Jesus
  Place of Last Supper
  Wall and Tower of King David
Pilate, 168, 194
Prayer, 131, 209, 223
Priesthood:
  Egypt, India, Persia, etc., 39-41
Projection, 206-209
Propaganda, 211-212
Psalms, Book of, 165

R

Raising of dead, 200-201
Reincarnation, 190
Resurrection: 137-138; 157, 166-167; 207
  Physical body, 185-191
Rituals (See Christian Church)

Roman officials, 102, 109
Rosicrucians: 22, 31, 130, **168**
  Explanation of, 232-235

S

Salvation, 191-192; 198, 211-212
Secret Teachings, 36-39; **74**
Sin, original, 220-221
Symbols, 53, 71, 86, 217

T

Teachings (See Secret Teachings)
Temple, meaning, 164
Theosophists, 31
Thomas, 155
Tiberias, 112
Tomb, Jesus, 137, 168-169
Trinity: 53
  Invented, 216-217
  Triune nature, 195-196
Twelve Disciples, 28

U

Upper room, 164

V

Vatican, 225, 228
Vowels:
  Christian use of, 128
  Pagan incantation, 127
  Prayer Chanting, 131-132

W

White magic, 123, 200
Wine:
  Symbol of, 117-119; 122, 139-140
  Water to, 210
Women, 18-19, 155-160
World War I, 206

Y

Young, Robert, 83

Explanatory

THE ROSICRUCIAN ORDER

ANTICIPATING questions which may be asked by the readers of this book, the publishers wish to announce that there is but one universal Rosicrucian Order existing in the world today, united in its various jurisdictions, and having one Supreme Council in accordance with the original plan of the ancient Rosicrucian manifestoes. The Rosicrucian Order is not a religious or sectarian society.

This international organization retains the ancient traditions, teachings, principles, and practical helpfulness of the Brotherhood as founded centuries ago. It is known as the *Ancient Mystical Order Rosae Crucis,* which name, for popular use, is abbreviated into AMORC. The Worldwide Jurisdiction of this Order has its headquarters at San Jose, California. Those interested in knowing more of the history and present-day helpful offerings of the Rosicrucians may have a *free* copy of the book entitled, *The Mastery of Life,* by sending a definite request to SCRIBE S.D.J. Rosicrucian Park, San Jose, California 95191, U.S.A.

The Rosicrucian Library

consists of a number of unique books which are described
in the following pages, and which may be
purchased from the

ROSICRUCIAN SUPPLY BUREAU
SAN JOSE, CALIFORNIA 95191, U.S.A.

▽ ▽ ▽

A THOUSAND YEARS OF YESTERDAYS

by H. Spencer Lewis, F.R.C., Ph.D.

This fascinating story dramatically presents the real facts of reincarnation. It explains how the soul leaves the body and *when* and *why* it returns to Earth again.

This revelation of the *mystic laws and principles* of the Masters of the East has never before been presented in such a form. Finely bound, and stamped in gold, it makes a fine addition to your library.

HERBALISM THROUGH THE AGES

by Ralph Whiteside Kerr, F.R.C.

The seemingly magical power of herbs endowed them with a divine essence to the mind of early man. Not only did they provide some of his earliest foods and become medicines for his illnesses but they also symbolized certain of his emotions and psychic feelings. This book presents the romantic history of herbs and their use even today.

EGYPT'S ANCIENT HERITAGE

by Rodman R. Clayson

Much of what we know today began in Egypt! Concepts that are unquestionably ancient show marvelous insights into natural law. From Egypt's mystery schools came rites and ceremonies that dramatize the creative Cosmic force. This book presents a masterly overview of the civilization of the Nile Valley.

ESSAYS OF A MODERN MYSTIC

by H. Spencer Lewis, F.R.C., Ph. D.

These private writings disclose the personal confidence and enlightenment that are born of *inner experience*. As a true mystic-philosopher, Dr. Lewis shares with his readers the results of contact with the Cosmic intelligence residing within.

MYSTICS AT PRAYER

Compiled by Many Cihlar

The first compilation of the famous prayers of the renowned mystics and adepts of all ages.

The book *Mystics at Prayer* explains in simple language the reason for prayer, how to pray, and the Cosmic laws involved. You come to learn the real efficacy of prayer and its full beauty dawns upon you. Whatever your religious beliefs, this book makes your prayers the application not of words, but of helpful, divine principles. You will learn the infinite power of prayer. Prayer is man's rightful heritage. It is the direct means of man's rightful heritage. It is the direct means of man's communion with the infinite force of divinity.

SELF MASTERY AND FATE WITH THE CYCLES OF LIFE

by H. Spencer Lewis, F.R.C., Ph. D.

This book demonstrates how to harmonize the self with the cyclic forces of each life.

Happiness, health and prosperity are available for those who know the periods in their own life that enhance the success of varying activities. Eliminate "chance" and "luck," cast aside "fate" and replace these with self mastery. Complete with diagrams and lists of cycles.

THE TECHNIQUE OF THE MASTER
THE WAY OF COSMIC PREPARATION

by Raymund Andrea, F.R.C.

A guide to inner unfoldment! The newest and simplest explanation for attaining the state of Cosmic Consciousness. To those who have felt the throb of a vital power within, and whose inner vision has at times glimpsed infinite peace and happiness, this book is offered. It converts the intangible whispers of self into forceful actions that bring real joys and accomplishments in life. It is a masterful work on psychic unfoldment.

THE SYMBOLIC PROPHECY OF THE GREAT PYRAMID

by H. Spencer Lewis, F.R.C., Ph. D.

The world's greatest mystery and first wonder is the Great Pyramid. Its history, vast wisdom and prophecies are all revealed in this beautifully bound and illustrated book. You will be amazed at the pyramid's scientific construction and at the secret knowledge of its mysterious builders.

LEMURIA—THE LOST CONTINENT OF THE PACIFIC

by Wishar S. Cervé

Where the Pacific now rolls in a majestic sweep for two thousand miles, there was once a vast continent known as Lemuria.

The scientific evidences of this lost race and its astounding civilization with the story of the descendants of the survivors present a cyclical viewpoint of rise and fall in the progress of civilization.

SON OF THE SUN

by Savitri Devi

The amazing story of Akhnaton (Amenhotep IV), Pharaoh of Egypt 1360 B.C. This is not just the fascinating story of one life—it is far more. It raises the curtain on man's emerging from superstition and idolatry. Against the tremendous opposition of a fanatical priesthood, Akhnaton brought about the world's first spiritual revolution. He was the first one to declare that there was a "sole God." In the words of Sir Flinders Petrie (*History of Egypt*): "Were it invented to satisfy our modern scientific conceptions, his religio-philosophy could not be logically improved upon at the present day."

This book contains over three hundred pages. It is handsomely printed, well bound, and stamped in gold.

THE MYSTICAL LIFE OF JESUS

by H. Spencer Lewis, F.R.C., Ph. D.

A full account of Jesus' life, containing the story of his activities in the periods not mentioned in the Gospel accounts, *reveals the real Jesus* at last.

This book required a visit to Palestine and Egypt to secure verification of the strange facts found in Rosicrucian records. Its revelations, predating the discovery of the Dead Sea Scrolls, show aspects of the Essenes unavailable elsewhere.

This volume contains many mystical symbols (fully explained), photographs, and an unusual portrait of Jesus.

THE SECRET DOCTRINES OF JESUS

by H. Spencer Lewis, F.R.C., Ph. D.

Even though the sacred writings of the Bible have had their contents scrutinized, judged and segments removed by twenty ecclesiastical councils since the year 328 A.D., there still remain buried in unexplained passages and parables the Great Master's *personal* doctrines.

Every thinking man and woman will find *hidden truths* in this book.

SEPHER YEZIRAH—A BOOK ON CREATION
OR THE JEWISH METAPHYSICS OF REMOTE ANTIQUITY

by Dr. Isidor Kalisch, Translator

The ancient basis for Kabalistic thought is revealed in this outstanding metaphysical essay concerning all creation. It explains the secret name of Jehovah.

Containing both the Hebrew and English texts, its 61 pages have been photolithographed from the 1877 edition. As an added convenience to students of Kabala, it contains a glossary of the original Hebraic words and terms.

MENTAL POISONING
THOUGHTS THAT ENSLAVE MINDS

by H. Spencer Lewis, F.R.C. Ph. D.

Must humanity remain at the mercy of evil influences created in the minds of the vicious? Do poisoned thoughts find innocent victims? Use the knowledge this book fearlessly presents as an antidote for such superstitions and their influences.

There is no need to remain helpless even though evil thoughts of envy, hate, and jealousy are aimed to destroy your self-confidence and peace of mind.

BEHOLD THE SIGN

by Ralph M. Lewis, F.R.C.

Unwrap the veil of mystery from the strange symbols inherited from antiquity. What were the *Sacred Traditions* said to be revealed to Moses? What were the discoveries of the Egyptian priesthood?

This book is fully illustrated with *age-old secret symbols* whose true meanings are often misunderstood. Even the mystical beginnings of the *secret signs* of many fraternal brotherhoods today are explained.

THE TECHNIQUE OF THE DISCIPLE

by Raymund Andrea, F.R.C.

The Technique of the Disciple is a book containing a modern description of the ancient esoteric path to spiritual Illumination, trod by the masters and avatars of yore. It has long been said that Christ left, as a great heritage to members of His secret council, a private method for guidance in life, which method has been preserved until today in the secret, occult, mystery schools.

Raymund Andrea, the author, reveals the method for attaining a greater life taught in these mystery schools, which perhaps parallels the secret instructions of Christ to members of His council. The book is informative, inspiring, and splendidly written. It is handsomely bound stamped in gold.

"UNTO THEE I GRANT..."

as revised by Sri Ramatherio

Out of the mysteries of the past comes this antique book that was written two thousand years ago, but was hidden in manuscript form from the eyes of the world and given only to the initiates of the temples in Tibet to study privately.

It can be compared only with the writings attributed to Solomon in the Bible of today. It deals with man's passions, weaknesses, fortitudes and hopes. Included is the story of the expedition into Tibet that secured the manuscript and the Grand Lama's permission to translate it.

THE BOOK OF JASHER
THE SACRED BOOK WITHHELD

What was written in this book of Holy Scripture that caused it to be expunged from the pages of the Bible? To what *veiled truths* were the prophets of old referring when they cried, "Is it not written in the Book of Jasher?"—Joshua 10:13, "Behold, it is written in the Book of Jasher" —II Samuel 1:18?

Read this photographic reproduction of the text whose rediscovery is credited to Alcuin, sage of Charlemagne's court.

COSMIC MISSION FULFILLED

by Ralph M. Lewis, F.R.C.

This illustrated biography of Harvey Spencer Lewis, Imperator of the Ancient, Mystical Order Rosae Crucis, was written in response to the requests of thousands of members who sought the key to this mystic-philosopher's life mission of rekindling the ancient flame of *Wisdom* in the Western world. We view his triumphs and tribulations from the viewpoint of those who knew him best.

Recognize, like him, that the present is our *moment in Eternity*; in it we fulfill our mission.

CONSCIOUS INTERLUDE

by Ralph M. Lewis, F.R.C.

With clarity of expression and insightful penetration of thought, this original philosopher leads us to contemplate such subjects as: the Fourth Dimension, the Mysteries of Time and Space; the Illusions of Law and Order; and many others of similar import.

As you follow the author through the pages into broad universal concepts, your mind too will feel its release into an expanding consciousness.

WHISPERINGS OF SELF

by Validivar

Wisdom, wit and insight combine in these brief aphorisms that derive from the interpretation of Cosmic impulses received by Validivar, whose true name is Ralph M. Lewis, Imperator of the Rosicrucian Order.

These viewpoints of all areas of human experience make an attractive gift as well as a treasured possession of your own.

ETERNAL FRUITS OF KNOWLEDGE

by Cecil A. Poole, F.R.C.

A stimulating presentation of philosophical insights that will provoke you into considering new aspects of such questions as: the purpose of human existence, the value of mysticism, and the true nature of good and evil. Paperback.

CARES THAT INFEST...

by Cecil A. Poole, F.R.C.

With a penetrating clarity, Cecil Poole presents us with the key to understanding our problems so that we may open wide the door and dismiss care from our lives. The author guides us on a search for *true value* so that, in the poet's words, "the night will be filled with music," as the *cares* "silently steal away."

ROSICRUCIAN MANUAL

by H. Spencer Lewis, F.R.C., Ph. D.

This practical book contains not only extracts from the Constitution of the Rosicrucian Order, but a complete outline and explanation of all the customs, habits, and terminology of the Rosicrucians, with diagrams and explanations of the symbols used in the teachings, an outline of the subjects taught, a dictionary of the terms, a complete presentation of the principles of Cosmic Consciousness, and biographical sketches of important individuals connected with the work. There are also special articles on the Great White Lodge and its existence, how to attain psychic illumination, the Rosicrucian Code of Life with twenty-nine laws and regulations, and a number of portraits of prominent mystics including Master K. H., the Illustrious.

The technical matter in the text and in the numerous diagrams makes this book a real encyclopedia of Rosicrucian explanations, aside from the dictionary of Rosicrucian terms.

The *Rosicrucian Manual* has been enlarged and improved since its first edition. Attractively bound, and stamped in gold.

MESSAGES FROM THE CELESTIAL SANCTUM

by Raymond Bernard, F.R.C.

The real *unity* is Cosmic Unity. No human being is separated from the Cosmic, no matter where he lives or how different his life style may be. Each person is like a channel through which cosmically inspired intuitive impressions and guidance can flow. The *Celestial Sanctum* in general is the universe. No earthly sanctuary is more sacred than the multiple phenomena which occur in the great extensions of the Cosmic. There are no greater Laws than those which operate this phenomenon.

This book explains how you can harmonize yourself with the *Celestial Sanctum*. Also, it reveals rational, sensible, and practical messages which were *cosmically* narrated. They can guide all, regardless of race or creed, toward a greater understanding and a complete mastery of one's life. Allow this book to explain to you how your mind can become like a window through which you can observe creation—and learn from it in a *personal way*.

MANSIONS OF THE SOUL

by H. Spencer Lewis, F.R.C., Ph. D.

Reincarnation: the world's most disputed doctrine! What did Jesus mean when he referred to the mansions in my Father's house? This book demonstrates what Jesus and his immediate followers knew about the rebirth of the soul, as well as what has been taught by sacred works and scholarly authorities in all parts of the world.

Learn about the cycles of the soul's reincarnations and how you can become acquainted with your present self and your past lives.

THE SANCTUARY OF SELF

by Ralph M. Lewis, F.R.C.

Are you living your life to your best advantage? Are you beset by a *conflict of desires*? Do you know that there are various *loves* and that some of them are dangerous drives?

Learn which of your feelings to discard as enslaving influences and which to retain as worthy incentives.

The author, Imperator of the Rosicrucian Order, brings to you from his years of experience, the practical aspects of mysticism.

ROSICRUCIAN PRINCIPLES FOR THE HOME AND BUSINESS

by H. Spencer Lewis, F.R.C., Ph. D.

This volume contains the practical application of Rosicrucian teachings to such problems as: ill health, common ailments, how to increase one's income or promote business propositions. It shows not only what to do, but what to avoid, in using metaphysical and mystical principles in starting and bringing into realization new plans and ideas.

Both business organizations and business authorities have endorsed this book.

ROSICRUCIAN QUESTIONS AND ANSWERS WITH COMPLETE HISTORY OF THE ORDER

by H. Spencer Lewis, F.R.C. Ph. D.

From ancient times to the present day, the history of the Rosicrucian Order is traced from its earliest traditional beginnings. Its historical facts are illuminated by stories of romance and mystery.

Hundreds of questions in this well-indexed volume are answered, dealing with the work, benefits and purposes of the Order.

MYSTICISM—THE ULTIMATE EXPERIENCE

by Cecil A. Poole, F.R.C.

An experience is more than just a sensation, a feeling. It is an *awareness,* or perception, with *meaning.* Our experiences are infinite in number, yet they are limited to certain types. Some are related to our objective senses; others, to dreams and inspirational ideas. But there is *one* that transcends them all—the *mystical experience.* It serves every category of our being: it stimulates, it enlightens, it strengthens; it is the *Ultimate Experience.*

And this book, *Mysticism—The Ultimate Experience,* defines it in simple and inspiring terms.

IN SEARCH OF REALITY

by Cecil A. Poole, F.R.C.

This Book Unites Metaphysics With Mysticism.

Man is not just an isolated entity on Earth. He is also of a great world—the Cosmos. The forces that create galaxies and island universes also flow through man's being. The human body and its vital phenomenon—Life—are of the same spectrum of energy of which all creation consists. The universe is you because you are one of its myriad forms of existence. Stripping away the mystery of this Cosmic relationship increases the personal reality of the Self.

YESTERDAY HAS MUCH TO TELL

by Ralph M. Lewis, F.R.C.

A personal account of witnessing primitive ceremonies, conversations with mystical teachers and austere high priests of the Near and Far East. It takes you to rites in the interior of Africa, and to temples in Peru, India, Egypt and other exotic lands. This is no mere travel book; the author was privileged, because of his Rosicrucian affiliation, to see and learn that which is not ordinarily revealed.

MENTAL ALCHEMY

by Ralph M. Lewis, F.R.C.

We can transmute our problems to workable solutions through *mental alchemy*. While this process is neither easy nor instantaneously effective, eventually the serious person will be rewarded. Certain aspects of our lives *can* be altered to make them more compatible with our goals.

Use this book to alter the direction of your life through proper thought and an understanding of practical mystical philosophy.

THROUGH THE MIND'S EYE

by Ralph M. Lewis, F.R.C.

Truth Is What Is Real To Us. Knowledge, experience, is the material of which truth consists. But what is the *real, the true,* of what we know? With expanding consciousness and knowledge, truth changes. Truth therefore is ever in the *balance*—never the same. But in turning to important challenging subjects, the *Mind's Eye* can extract that which is the true and the real, for the *now*. The book, *Through The Mind's Eye,* calls to attention important topics for judgment by your mind's eye.

THE CONSCIENCE OF SCIENCE
and Other Essays

by Walter J. Albersheim, Sc.D., F.R.C.

A remarkable collection of fifty-four essays by one of the most forthright writers in the field of science and mysticism. His frank and outspoken manner will challenge readers to look again to their own inner light, as it were, to cope with the ponderous advances in modern technology.

ORDER BOOKS FROM
ROSICRUCIAN SUPPLY BUREAU
ROSICRUCIAN PARK, SAN JOSE, CALIFORNIA 95191, U.S.A.

For a complete, illustrated catalogue and price list
of the books listed herein, please write to the
Rosicrucian Supply Bureau.